THE CULTURAL SIGNIFICANCE OF THE REFORMATION

Perseverate

Fonda

THE CULTURAL
SIGNIFICANCE OF
THE REFORMATION

Karl Holl

Introduction by Wilhelm Pauck

Translated by Karl and Barbara Hertz
and John H. Lichtblau

LIVING AGE BOOKS
published by MERIDIAN BOOKS, INC. *New York*

KARL HOLL

Karl Holl was born in Tübingen, Germany, on May 15, 1866. He was professor of church history in Tübingen and in Berlin, where he died on May 23, 1926. His collected works have been published in Germany in three large volumes, divided as follows: I.: Luther; II.: the Eastern Church; III.: the Western Church.

Translated by Karl and Barbara Hertz and John H. Lichtblau from the German original, *"Die Kulturbedeutung der Reformation,"* in *Gesammelte Aufsätze zur Kirchengeschichte,* Vol. I (J. C. B. Mohr [Paul Siebeck]; Tübingen, 1948). The text dates from 1911, but was revised by the author after the First World War.

M

A Living Age Books Original
First published by Meridian Books, Inc., November 1959

First printing October 1959

CONTENTS

INTRODUCTION
by Wilhelm Pauck

The author of the following work, Karl Holl (1866-1926), was professor of church history in the University of Berlin (1906-26). As such he was the immediate colleague of Adolf von Harnack. Although the two men were different in temperament (Harnack was open and versatile, diplomatic and tolerant, while Holl was very strict in the demands he made of himself and of others, hence tending to be diffident and severe), they were close friends who co-operated beautifully with one another. Harnack, fifteen years older than Holl, was at the height of world-wide influence and fame when Holl came from the University of Tübingen to Berlin, and for some years Harnack overshadowed

his colleague and friend. But in the years immediately after the First World War, when Harnack had reached retirement age, Holl suddenly
began to exercise a deep impact upon Christian
thought. An ever-growing number of students
flocked to his lectures and he was hailed as a
widely influential thinker. The immediate cause
of this was the fact that, in 1921, he had begun
to publish his collected essays. They were all
scholarly articles, research papers, or academic
orations, dealing with a wide range of church-
historical subjects. Although not easily acces-
sible (some were published in the Proceedings
of the Berlin Academy of Sciences, of which
Holl had become a member in 1915), these
writings were already famous in academic circles, for almost without exception they were
highly original and executed with an amazing
scholarly skill. Holl was a master of languages;
wherever possible, he used the primary sources
and studied and interpreted them according to
the strictest rules of philological criticism. It
was characteristic of him that, as a man of
mature years, he insisted on learning Russian
in order to be able to read original texts per-
taining to the Eastern Orthodox Church. Two
volumes (one dealing with Eastern Christianity
from Paul to Tolstoy and the other with Western Christianity from Tertullian to Mary Baker
Eddy) were published only in 1928, two years

after Holl's death, but according to his plans. They had been preceded by a large volume, first published in 1921 and reissued with revisions in 1923, devoted entirely to a study of various phases of the thought and teaching of Martin Luther. Here were thorough and extended treatments of such themes as the following: Luther's understanding of the nature and meaning of religion; Luther's reconstruction of Christian ethics; Luther's judgments of himself; Luther's significance for the history and development of exegesis and hermeneutics; the cultural significance of the Reformation.

This volume made Holl famous almost overnight. Its influence was and still is very great, despite the fact that it was never intended to make a ready and wide appeal. It contained intricate discussions on difficult theological themes like justification and predestination. The writing was clear and direct in style, but it was also filled with innumerable complicated footnotes in small print, in which the German and Latin words of Luther and his interpreters were reproduced exactly as they had been written or spoken in the sixteenth century. The author plainly wished his writing to be read as that of a historian engaged in the effort to understand Luther's thought and work in the context of the sixteenth century, but, at the same time, he conveyed to his readers a sense of urgency about the validity of Luther's thought that made them regard his exposition as being of utmost importance for contemporary religion and theology.

Holl's Luther essays affected the theological discussion of our times at three points: (1) they steadied the thinking of many who had been thrown off balance by the violent criticisms that Barth and his friends leveled against liberal theology; (2) they came quickly to be regarded as the climax of a fresh interest in the theological thought of Martin Luther, which had been developing for several years, inaugurating the so-called Luther renaissance in contemporary Protestantism; (3) they were addressed to historical problems that Max Weber and Ernst Troeltsch in particular had raised about the interrelations between religion and culture and about the significance of the Reformation for the rise of modern civilization.

The work here offered for the first time in English translation is of special interest because of its relevance to the third point, and this we must therefore discuss in more detail. But in view of the fact that it presupposes Holl's basic conception of Luther's theological thought, a few words about the other two points will not be out of place.

(1) Karl Barth's *The Epistle to the Romans* and the other writings that came from his pen between 1918 and 1925 had dealt such a blow

to the anthropocentric and humanistic side of liberal theology and to the historical method on which it relied that there was considerable consternation in the camp of its adherents. Harnack called Barth a despiser of scientific (i.e., historically critical) theology and expressed his utter surprise at the fact that he who in his historical work had found himself able to understand or to make sense out of many types of theological thought appeared to lack an aerial that would enable him to receive the Barthian ideas. He and his friends (and also many of his followers and students) feared that Barth would do great harm to the Christian gospel in the modern world if his apparent attempt to free Protestant theology from the method of historical criticism should prove successful. In this situation Holl's work on Luther showed to many a way out of the difficulty. It was the ripe fruit of strict historical studies and as such a product of modern Protestant historical theology. At the same time it presented a plea (entirely by the weight and power of its argument) for the renewal of Luther's faith in modern Protestantism. And this faith was shown to be theocentric and thus utterly different from any form of humanism. Moreover, it was defined as directed solely to the gospel of the forgiveness of sin and as such utterly different from all religions and religious practices that live by the notion that only people who have proved themselves worthy of God's holiness are acceptable in his sight. In other words, Holl's method and argument seemed to constitute an important medium between Barthianism and liberal theology. On this account it was warmly welcomed by many who could not swallow Barth's neo-orthodoxy but were critical of the liberals because they seemed to them to lack religious depth and were therefore unable to understand the gospel as the divine promise of forgiveness to the sinner. It was therefore not surprising that Holl was criticized alike by Barth and unrepentant liberals. However, these very criticisms kept his book alive. (The German text is now in its seventh edition, published in 1948.)

(2) A very important phase of contemporary Protestantism is the deep interest shown by many in the thought of the Reformers. This interest is not merely historical. The Reformers, and especially Luther and Calvin, are being studied passionately with the expectation that they will be able to say a creative and saving word to Christians of today. Many excellent and profound books have been written about Luther's teaching in recent years and they have made his thought so relevant to the needs of our day that this concern for him represents a veritable Luther-renaissance. It was stimulated

chiefly by two factors: the modern custom of celebrating anniversaries of great men of the past, and the discovery and publication of important writings of the *young* Luther.

Luther became an exceedingly prominent beneficiary of the modern passion to commemorate great men and their achievements by the celebration of anniversaries. Since October 31, 1917, when, despite the war, the whole Protestant world commemorated the beginning of the Reformation through Luther's publication of the Ninety-five Theses on Indulgences, until February 18, 1946, when the four hundredth anniversary of Luther's death was observed, all important events in the Reformer's life and every achievement of his labors have been interpreted to modern men in hundreds of books and commentaries. Our generation is better informed about him and the course of the Protestant Reformation than any other of former ages, including that of the Reformation itself. Holl's Luther essays played an important role in all this. They defined the problems for many other students of Luther and set the tone for their studies. Moreover, they were so original and at the same time so powerful that they remained unmatched; indeed, they are still fresh today and will not be outdated for a long time. Holl concentrated his attention upon the young Luther, and he succeeded in showing clearly from the sources what Luther's motivations were and what they remained throughout his career. Furthermore, in his interpretation of Luther, he disregarded or bypassed many of the scenes and events that confined the Reformer to his own time and place, and he chose to illuminate those aspects of his thought and life which set off his particular comprehension of the gospel from that of other Christian thinkers.

(3) In *The Cultural Significance of the Reformation* Holl makes frequent reference to the works of Weber and Troeltsch. The very theme of this study seems to have been suggested by Max Weber's investigation of the relation between "the Protestant ethic and the spirit of capitalism" and by Ernst Troeltsch's treatment of the connection between Protestantism and modern civilization in his book on "the significance of the Reformation for the development of modern civilization" (which in the English translation is called *Protestantism and Progress*) and particularly in his large work *The Social Teaching of the Christian Churches*.

These epoch-making studies, which are still the subject of many fruitful discussions, must be seen against the background of two characteristically modern interests. In the first place, they represent the reaction of two famous thinkers to the Marxist view of history. Although not partisan works, they were designed to show that a good case can be made for the shaping influence of religious ideas upon political, social, and economic factors of life. Indeed they were nothing else than detailed historical investigations of the interrelation between religion and civilization. In the second place, these books—and particularly those by Troeltsch—must be appreciated in connection with the inquiry that has been carried on since the Enlightenment and is still the explicit or implicit preoccupation of all thinkers concerned with the philosophical or cultural interpretation of history: the inquiry about the importance of the Reformation and of Protestantism for the rise and development of modern civilization.

The concern of the men of the Enlightenment for human freedom and autonomy developed the notion that the Reformation of Martin Luther marked the beginning of the "modern era," because one felt that Luther's so-called rediscovery of the gospel and his assaults upon the papacy had brought about the breakup of the authoritarianism of the papacy and of the Roman Catholic Church. During the American and French revolutions it was frequently asserted that the struggle for liberty in which men were engaged was somehow a continuation of the protest of Martin Luther against the authority of the papacy. The historians of the nineteenth century took it for granted that the "modern age" began with the Reformation, and in the twentieth century this idea became so universal that even Roman Catholic historians felt compelled to undertake the proof that the so-called crises of "modern civilization" were the end result of the revolt of Luther and the Protestant Reformers against the faith and order of the papal Church. However, it was never easy to support general judgments of this kind by convincing historical evidence. Hence it was of highest significance that when, in 1906, Ernst Troeltsch was asked to substitute for Max Weber (who was ill) to deliver a lecture before a congress of historians on Protestantism and the spirit of the modern age, he chose to point out as objectively as possible that although the rise of the modern world must be understood in terms of the attitudes engendered by the Renaissance and the Reformation and that although Protestantism produced and continues to shape the religious spirit of modern Western civilization, the factors that really determine modern civilization —secularized political power and technological economic power, made possible by the historical sense and by the discoveries and investigations of the natural sciences—must be interpreted as being in opposition to the Reformation and to Protestantism. In other words, Troeltsch argued that modern civilization had *two* special beginnings—in the Reformation, which effected the emancipation of powerful cultural forces from the papacy, and in the spirit of the nineteenth century which, formed by the Enlightenment, emancipated common life from the authority of organized religion, including that of Protestantism.

Anyone who wishes fully to understand the setting of Holl's inquiry about the cultural significance of the Reformation must consult Troeltsch's lecture. He will find that Holl—who covers practically the same ground as Troeltsch—gives different judgments and comes to different conclusions. Holl does not choose to deal with the general historical problem of the extent to which the modern world still is dependent upon Protestantism, but he undertakes the task to specify as concretely as possible where and how the Reformation formed cultural attitudes. He does so under the auspices of a somewhat indefinite title: *The Cultural Significance* [*Kulturbedeutung*] *of the Reformation*. He does not appear to share Troeltsch's negative and critical judgment about the secularization of modern life, although he does not directly and specifically reject it, but he leaves the over-all impression that he would not mind being counted among those early moderns who were sure that Luther inaugurated the modern world.

Moreover, Holl seems to be concerned to demonstrate the cultural effects of the Reformation by proofs or interpretations that are specific. The scope of his knowledge and the thoroughness of his acquaintance with widely spread literary sources certainly are most impressive. One can see how many fruitful investigations in the field of religion and culture can be undertaken and should still be made. Yet one will also notice how precarious such an inquiry is. Even a master like Holl can frequently be observed in the commission of two basic faults that beset many a historian: he often does not appear to have taken into consideration all the concrete environmental factors to which the ideas and attitudes he discusses were related. Furthermore, he discloses very sharply the biased opinions and prejudices that informed his thinking. This is made especially evident in the discussion of political matters. There he shows himself a German patriot who tended to idealize his own people and as a nationalist who seems not to have sensed that many of his judgments which he regarded as historically correct and morally sound were inspired by a provincial conviction that his country could do no wrong.

It is because even the noblest historians commit such errors of judgment that history must be rewritten again and again. Today many people are eager to learn more about the interrelations between religion and culture and specifically between Protestant Christianity and modern civilization. Perhaps the publication of Holl's essay in an English translation will stimulate such investigations. Undertaken from a competence comparable to his, they will demonstrate how deeply and searchingly he could probe.

May 1959

I. RELIGION AND

SECULAR LIFE

Anyone undertaking to examine the topic I have selected finds himself immediately confronted with a basic problem. It was Spengler who wrote the sober words: "A ruler who attempts to impose religion in terms of practical political aims is a fool. A moralist who wants to bring to the real world truth, justice, peace, and good will is also a fool. No religion has ever changed THE WORLD and no empirical fact has ever disproved religion."

There is no doubt that at one time this view expressed the general attitude among historians. Even if one refuses to go along with Karl Marx in reducing religion and all other "ideologies" to strictly economic processes, there is still a tendency to regard the laws of political and economic development as autonomous and independent of those of morality and religion. Of course, no serious researcher will deny that religion at certain turning points, as for example during the Reformation, had a deep impact on the course of history. The facts speak for themselves. But according to this view, religion was only one of several factors. The decisive influence in all such cases, it is held, was not religion but economic and political circumstances. Religious faith, according to this view, creates a world of its own to which everybody may react as he pleases. But the person truly oriented to reality has never acted on its basis, and if he seemed to do so he only fooled himself. According to this approach, it is the function of the exact sciences, which concern themselves not with the dreams but with the real motivations of men, to uncover this sober truth also in the course of history.[1] True, at the dawn of history there was evidence of a powerful religious force. But, as everyone knows since Comte, true progress in civilization takes place through emancipation from religion. By the time of the Renaissance the relationship between religion and civilization has undergone a complete change. From now on it is civilization which promotes religion. While religion is permitted to retain a certain degree of independence it now becomes the servant of secular strivings and glorifies progress by superimposing its spirituality on it. At any rate, these historians say, creative force does not originate from it, but from the constantly rising tide of secularism.

A different view is expressed by Max Weber in his famous essay on the spirit of capitalism. His attempt to prove that something apparently so far removed as the structure of the contemporary economy stems from religious inspiration did not fail to make an impact. One may venture to predict that the generalization of these concepts, which Weber undertook in his essays about the economic ethics of world religions, will continue to mold contemporary thinking. However, so far, Weber's interpretations have been concerned far more with specific cases than with their basic premises. Thus the question still remains whether religion has sufficient force to transform and improve man, and whether the power it generates is strong enough to withstand and overcome the "natural," i.e., the economic, sociological, and political forces.

Bearing this question in mind, it is surprising to discover that Luther's views on this point are not very different from those of Spengler. Had one asked Luther if his gospel intended to advance civilization he would have replied with a resounding No. He would, no doubt, have explained with the same decisiveness that he used with the peasants when he said: "My gospel has nothing to do with the things of this world. It is something unique, exclusively concerned with souls. To promote and settle the affairs of this temporal life is not a duty of my office, but of those called to this work, the emperor, the nobility, the magistrates. And the source upon which they must draw is not the gospel, but reason, tradition, and equity."

Indeed, Luther wanted above all to re-awaken in his contemporaries an awareness of the independence and autonomous significance of religion. Religion is to him not only the supreme value, the peak and summation of all other life values which must, of course, be utilized as a means toward an end other than itself—be it cultural achievements, world domination, or the art of living. It is, in fact, not a "value" at all, in the conventional meaning of the term. Luther sees religion as founded on a self-contained relationship, on an "ought to," an original obligation stemming from the gift of life itself, deepened by the sacrifice of Christ, unaltered by any temporal condition.

Yet, at the same time, what does it mean that Luther assigns the management of secular affairs to "reason"? Do Luther's views in this, too, coincide with Spengler's? Does he also—though for a different reason than Spengler, namely despair of the world—leave free rein to drive for power and hedonism, tempered only by utilitarian considerations and enlightened self-interest?

Luther has, indeed, been widely interpreted

in this manner, but such interpretations indicate a gross misunderstanding. Had Luther meant this he would have deserted the basic meaning of his ethics, which states that <u>faith has to assert itself in the hard reality[2] of everyday life.</u> However, this was not the case. True, Luther perceives life with a sober view and realizes full well how—given the conditions of existence on earth—man strives first of all for gratification of his desire for happiness and welfare. Nor is he inclined to damn such desires.[3] Furthermore, he recognizes that the individual's clamor for happiness unavoidably gives rise to controversy, which requires the establishment of civil order, and he praises reason, which can install and uphold such order. Moreover, he understands that such systems created by human reason, especially political states, must continue their existence also under Christianity. The gospel cannot and does not want to supersede them. For the gospel can only reach those of good will, those willing to receive God and thus by their very nature of good will, while the secular order must deal with all, the crude, the unfeeling, and the criminal included. Also, civil institutions require specialists with diverse qualifications that cannot be acquired by the teachings of the gospel. <u>The gospel teaches how to win and guide souls, but one can no more learn from it how to</u>

govern a state than how to practice a trade.

However, with all that Luther has not yet uttered his last word about reason. If he ascribes to it the function of ordering civil affairs, he does not thereby exclude the possibility that reason, too, is affected by a deeper driving force. Moreover, he demands that deeper driving force from the Christian. For, though the interrelations in state and economy are primarily of a judiciary and business nature, they are, nevertheless, based on human relationships that obligate the Christian to exercise his unconditional duty to love.[4]

Thus love sets a still higher goal for human relationships than the mutual benefits to be derived from co-operation for the common good or the greatest happiness.[5] For Christian love teaches us to recognize the neighbor in one's fellow man. Thereby, reason is lifted onto a higher level. And Luther recognizes only that reason as true in which love is present as the guiding force. Reason in this true meaning becomes co-equal with such concepts as equity, consideration, protection; in other words, the seeking of a personal community above the impersonal soberness of judiciary administration. Yet, the aim is not to supersede the secular order, but rather to ennoble it and convert its original harshness into something humane.

Likewise, Luther rejects the worship of "personality" as the highest aim of culture. He sees the true duty of civilization as resting with man himself, yet not with man as an individual, though he is fully aware of the importance of the individual. It is the relationship of man to man which Luther sees as the highest reward of the community.

This interpretation does not invalidate Luther's pronouncements about the gospel and its relationship to the world. Civilization always remains a secular aim beneath that of the true and highest kingdom of God. Even in its most idealized form civilization can never become identical with the kingdom of God, much less take its place. Nevertheless, according to Luther work toward such an idealized society is a Christian duty. Moreover, in Lutheran meaning only a Christian can seriously seek such a goal and only a Christian can strive toward it with all his might. For love, which must be the driving force, can only have endurance if it is constantly renewed by the consciousness of the union with God.

Luther thus demanded that the effects of Christian love become manifest in man and the secular order. Did this demand falter owing to the self-contained causality of secular affairs, or was Luther himself proof that genuine culture is only created by one who knows a still higher value?

In order to answer these questions one must first form a concept of how the motivations that Luther gained from his relationship to God affected his worldly activities. From his understanding of the gospel Luther threw two major ideas as active forces into the stream of culture: a new concept of personality and a new concept of community.

Luther's concept of personality is rooted in that sense of responsibility which through his work was given a heightened significance. When he considered the Last Judgment it dawned on him that, just as the relationship between God and man is a completely unmediated one, so, too, the responsibility for one's own actions and intentions cannot be thrust off on any other person, not even on a priest. The discovery of the doctrine of justification elevated the independence of the individual, which was based on this relationship to God, to an even higher level. From the unconstrained sense of unity with God, Luther now derives, in addition, the right and obligation of the believer to act even without the compulsion of law, i.e., out of his individual sense of the divine will to produce by his own creative act the proper form of morality in a specific instance. Luther thereby expands the right of the individual personality to a degree unheard of—except in Paul—but he attaches to it an obligation of responsibility of equal weight. By uniting the two ideas he parts company with the opinion accepted as pious in the Catholic Church as well as with the Renaissance idea of personality. His view of personality struck directly at the avoidance of responsibility by the Catholic faithful, but it struck in no lesser degree at a superman concept which disregarded conscience and relied upon the power of innate drives and the right of the stronger. Against both he argued the principle that the magnitude of the responsibility determines the stature of the personality.

But to emphasize this personal obligation immediately altered the position of the individual within the existing political and social order. However sharply Luther might otherwise oppose the idea that political or economic freedoms could be derived from a religious relationship, from "the freedom of the Christian man"—in this he saw a clouding of the issues, an abuse of religion for selfish ends—he was forced to assert unequivocally this one point, that freedom of conscience, the right of personal conviction in religious matters, was something clearly inviolable. Here he had to insist that it was even the duty of the individual person to resist every pressure from without, at least in so far as his inner life would be thereby affected. For the salvation of every individual hung in the balance here. If the religion that an individual practiced was only one forced on him, practiced under coercion, then it was one that was false for him personally, a hypocritical religion. God did not desire compulsory service. And if the individual had the duty to defend this fundamental right against an oppressing church, he had a double duty to defend it against the state and society.[6] Thus within the existing order based on authority and force there appears something autonomous, something hard and unyielding, on which that order will either break or be forced to change.

But Luther's concept of personality reached further than this, even into economic life. Luther considered it inherent in the nature of the man reborn in God that he found his joy in activity. Just as for Luther God is the eternally creative and active being, and the faith of man is "the vital, creative, active, powerful thing, which works unceasingly and is ever busy," so according to him the Christian is drawn into activity everywhere. The true Christian cannot be idle; or if he is, his conscience bothers him.[7] The "old Adam" is indeed a loafer who always wants force and driving.[8] For he belongs to the world, and the world does not suspect the blessing of work. The Christian's advantage, on the other hand, is that he works with an inner zest. Luther thereby elevates "work for the sake of work" to a Christian principle.

It is necessary, however, to distinguish his concept clearly from later distortions. Luther derived the impulse to work exclusively from his dynamic conception of the living God without adding further refinements of motivation, such as, e.g., the so-called "testing of faith." For the mature Luther the ascetic value of work is also no longer the decisive basis of determination. The most important point in this connection is that Luther, despite his high praise of work in itself, takes a position as far away as possible from an uninspired busy-ness that is indifferent to the content of work. He stresses (cf. the "Sermon on Good Works") just this fact, that the worker is always conscious of the meaning of his work. The certainty that work is worthwhile, that it really serves God and one's neighbor, calls forth the complete inner joy in work which Luther demands.

This evaluation of work leads Luther even further to the development of a corresponding concept of honor. That pride of Paul's—who would not be dependent on the gifts of his congregations, but would rather earn the necessities of life by the work of his own hands—is reawakened in Luther.[9] According to him, the Christian also manifests his own worth and his independence in that he does not live at the expense of others, does not depend upon their generosity on his behalf, even if they are Christian brethren, but he will work himself in order, whenever possible, to give something of his own to others.[10] This thought touched closely on points of view which had developed in the towns among the rising bourgeoisie. But the religious basis, which Luther gave his idea, first gave this concept its overpowering impetus. The Reformation could decisively take up the battle against mendicancy only because for it mendicancy had lost that religious status that the Catholic Church had provided.

Still a third trait characterizes Luther's view of work. He wants work to be ordered, i.e., to be activity in a calling. Luther changed not only the content of the word "calling"; he recoined the word itself. What is new is that in his mature years, he sees the "call" of God exclusively in secular duties, i.e., he unites just those two elements which for Catholic thought were contradictions that could scarcely coexist. Only timidly had the viewpoint dared to present itself in Catholicism that one could also heed the call of God in the world and in secular work. But by decisively including secular activities under this exalted viewpoint as a God-given obligation, Luther diverts to it all the religious energy that heretofore was exhausted and fragmented in "good works" alongside work in a vocation. On the other hand, he also introduces into work the consciously purposive. The piece of work that the individual performs is only a small part of the total enterprise that the various vocations in co-operation with one another carry out for the common good. But it is indispensable in its place and it fulfills its purpose only when it is done faithfully and devotedly with an eye to the supreme good.

Together with this richly developed concept of personality Luther set up a concept of community elaborated with equal sharpness.

What community really means became clear to Luther as he framed his concept of the church. In this form, the form of a church—not the visible but the invisible, in the kingdom of God—he sees the highest achievement that could be imagined as the goal of human association. For this community is (these are for him the decisive identifying characteristics) simultaneously perfectly free and yet most intimate and productive. Through the Word of God, which has become powerful in their hearts, the members are gathered together without coercion; the choicest treasure has been given them, yet they never attain perfection in it; and thus they are impelled of themselves to a spiritual exchange, to a constant giving and receiving. Luther tore this invisible church free from all temporal forms, specifically also from equating it with the visible Catholic Church. But it does not, therefore, in his thinking dissolve it into a mere intellectual concept. It exists right now as a tangible reality, supporting the individual member. Every believer has the right to feel himself a member and also the duty to practice the corresponding will for community face to face with his fellow human being.

The blunt and unyielding quality of the love commandment of the New Testament becomes clear to Luther in its relationship to this principle. Luther restored the original meaning of this commandment and thereby accomplished a breach in the Catholic tradition no less important than his distinction between the visible and the invisible church. He interprets the prescriptions of the Sermon on the Mount as strict commandments, which affect every Christian, and he clears away all the rubbish of qualifications, dispensations, and preferential treatment under which the Catholic Church had buried the simple grandeur of these demands. But Luther presses on to the heart of the issue with the sharply put question whether it was possible for self-love to exist along with or even prior to the love of neighbor demanded there. Contrary to the scholastics and also to Augustine, he decided that the word of Jesus to the scribes—"Thou shalt love thy neighbor as thyself"—was not meant to say, as the Catholic Church interpreted it, that self-love was something equally justified or even prerequisite for love of one's neighbor, but that love of self should be replaced by love of neighbor. Thus the whole concept of love was changed. Love of one's neighbor thus did not arise out of the mellowing of self-love or through an expansion of the ego, which eventually perhaps might include all mankind. It was a break with self-love; in place of the individual ego, the community became primary; only within it did the individual find himself and indeed find himself as a serving member. Thus conceived, the concept of love was closely related to that of the invisible church. The invisible church was the community that existed prior to the individual, which he must recognize as set over him. And if it was an obligation of faith to approach every person with the prejudgment that he belonged to this church or was divinely destined for it, then even the heavy sacrifices that the Sermon on the Mount demanded appeared only as a self-evident proof of the mutual commitment that one brother owed another.

But—and this, too, distinguishes him from Catholic tradition—Luther simultaneously introduced reflection, judgment, and awareness of purpose into the practice of love. If he quite earnestly expects that on the basis of the letter of the gospel one should give an adversary not only one's cloak, but also one's coat, he does not, therefore, mean that one must throw it after the thug. The injured person is obligated to confront the robber with his crime.[11] Love makes precisely this demand of him. Similarly, Luther could only disapprove the indiscriminate giving of alms even to the shiftless, which only encouraged their indolence,[12] or depriving one's family of necessities to help others[13]—an admonition which Luther, by the way, with some reason could have directed toward himself.[14] Luther does not set these qualifications in order to weaken the unconditional nature of the command once again; by these very qualifications he intends rather for the first time to set the commandment in its proper focus. He wants to emphasize a simple truth, constantly forgotten in both Eastern and Western Catholicism, namely, that love only merits its name when it keeps its goal clearly in view: to be of real help to the other person and to improve his condition, spiritually, too, if possible. Neither a comfortable tolerance that allowed everything to pass over it, nor a generosity that dis-

tributed its goods thoughtlessly would suffice
for this. Even when it gives in, love must act
decisively and its gifts must, as Luther expresses himself, "flow out of faith," [15] i.e.,
love must know what it wishes to accomplish
with its gifts. Luther adds a further observation to this last point, in which the full sensitivity of his perceptions is revealed. He liked
to use the expression that in love one was permitted to become "god" for another. But he
used the same catchword to identify the danger
lurking in every act of love.[16] He had a clear
awareness that the benevolence of the donor
always led him into the temptation to pose as
"god" to the other, i.e., to consider himself
superior and to oppress the other or even to
make him his dependent. To give "simply" so
that one forgets one's self in the other seemed
to him a fine art that would only be learned
through strict self-discipline.

These fundamental ideas of Luther have become the common property of the whole movement flowing from him. Not only Zwingli and
Calvin adopted them, but also—a point needing
special emphasis today—the "enthusiasts" and
the "sects." The enthusiasts cannot be named
along with Luther as independent spirits. They
themselves acknowledged their dependence on
Luther, inasmuch as they accused him of
stopping halfway in his reformation. Therein

lay the involuntary admission that they had learned from Luther the principles that they emphasized. As a matter of fact, they were under obligation to him not only for the liberation from the papacy—in itself no small matter —but also for their conception of personality and for their interpretation of the Sermon on the Mount as well. Although they might undergird their concept of personality, not as Luther did by the doctrine of justification, but mystically or rationally, the decisive fact is still that the themes which they emphasized—responsibility, autonomy, certainty of salvation— came from Luther, not from mysticism. Even more evident is their relationship to Luther in their concept of the love commandment. They could not derive the radicalism with which they demanded the fulfillment of what this commandment required from the limping interpretations of Erasmus or from the evaluation of the Sermon on the Mount by the medieval sects. Luther first opened their eyes to the meaning of the New Testament commandment, and his enthusiasm kindled their zeal. Even what the Anabaptists made out of Luther's views, whether he approved or not, belongs among the influences of the Reformation.

But still another factor has to be considered if one wants to understand the historic manifestation of these principles in their specific form. A certain inner tension exists between the concept of personality and that of community. Luther sensed this and counteracted it. It is precisely where his personality concept reaches its peak and therefore tends to conflict most with the community concept—where the idea of the "strong" comes in—that he emphasizes the obligation of the strong to adapt himself to the community in order to use his talents to help the weak. Of course, in reality it proved extremely difficult to achieve the correct balance between these conflicting forces. The concept of personality, appearing from the beginning as the stronger and increasing in significance by its contrast with Catholicism, could therefore be turned *against* the concept of community, to weaken or even completely to dissolve it, as happened among the great individualists, most conclusively in the instance of Sören Kierkegaard. Lutheranism was particularly endangered because the church, the chosen representative of the concept of community, never developed a position of power alongside the state. But Calvinism, too, at least in part, experienced this danger during a specific stage of its development.

II. EFFECTS ON POLITICAL

AND ECONOMIC LIFE

The implication of the new principles became apparent first of all and most notably over against the state. In their encounter with it, two effects resulted: on the one hand, a deepening of the theory of the state; on the other hand, a definite limitation of its powers.

The new principles shattered, first of all, the argument on the basis of which the church had up to that time denied the state the right of complete autonomy. The church derived its authority to keep a watch over the state from the fact that as the guardian of revelation also in those questions of morality which were recognized as the highest purpose of the state, the questions of right and justice, it possessed the final decisive verdict. The doctrine of the universal priesthood, of the right and duty of the believer to a personal responsibility, destroyed this prerogative that the church had claimed. The truths of Christian morality are not entrusted to one specific estate alone for protection; just as they bind every Christian, so they are also clear and explicit for each individual. Why should not then a Christian government—for obviously only in the instance of a Christian government can there be an issue of the relationship to the church—be qualified to apply these principles independently to the circumstances it encounters just as well as every individual Christian is entitled and obligated to judge the situations of his calling?

Luther, of course, could not be satisfied with demonstrating the state's independence of the church. Behind it there arises for him—based on his concept of community—the further question of the justification of the state as such. Today it is particularly noteworthy that it was Luther who first [1] concerned himself keenly with this issue, which is of such significance to our time. The first Christians had no need to concern themselves with this problem. Jesus could limit himself to define the different code of behavior which held for his disciples, without the need to fight or defend the state itself. Augustine, too, attacked only the big state, but did not oppose the small state limited to the confines of a single people.

For Luther this question became one of fundamental urgency. For, on the one hand, he was like the purest of the early Christians in finding the essence of the highest community, the kingdom of God, in love, voluntary acts, and selfless mutual assistance. Yet, on the other hand, he lived in a period when not only the big states but also the small, and even minute ones, displayed evidence of external expansionist desires and internal autocratic trends. All this gave him a most vivid picture of the friction between these two forms of community.

Nevertheless, Luther did not answer the question in the spirit of the Anabaptists. In order to co-ordinate the concept of the kingdom of God with that of the state he had to go back to the most profound aspects of Christianity. Faced with this question it was not enough to point out that the state is indispensable for the world and the preservation of its goods and that the system thus created, though inadequate in specific instances, does constitute an order whose reasonableness calls for approval. For what reason may find acceptable is not necessarily justifiable for the Christian.

Especially in matters of ethics, the Christian has good cause to mistrust mere "reason." It was also not quite satisfactory to stress, as Luther did, that the gospel had validity for only a part of humanity and could therefore never become a universal system. For this gave rise to the impression that the need for the state arose from a weakness of the gospel.

Thus if the state were to withstand the scrutiny of the Christian conscience, Luther had to give a positive reason why a secular order was important for the kingdom of God. This was the point at which Luther took up the issue. He found the justification for the state in the fact that God's kingdom has to expand and develop in this world. "In this world" means within a humanity, more than half of which proved itself inaccessible to the highest form of ethics. In this situation the state comes to the assistance of the kingdom of God by protecting its otherwise helpless members—and therewith also the members of Christianity—from annihilation by a ruthless and selfish majority. Through the maintenance of peace and order the state secures the undisturbed preaching of the gospel and through its dispensation of justice, based on the concept of equity, it simultaneously paves the way for the acceptance of the gospel.

On its highest level the state is for Luther not an end in itself, but only a means toward the absolute. Yet, this function gives the state great dignity, since, at least as far as earthly things are concerned, it is indispensable, and next to the church, the most important means toward the absolute.

Nowadays such a view is often called "medieval." But one can only call it so if one considers every inclusion of the religious view-point "medieval." Actually, Luther transcended the Middle Ages with this concept in more than one way. For one thing, Luther's higher order, for whose service the state exists, is no longer the visible church but the kingdom of God; against the visible church the state retains its independence. The representatives of the church can in matters of ethics urge and advise and influence public opinion, but they cannot enforce anything by religious means. Furthermore, by securing the justification of the state in terms of a positive religious goal Luther went beyond all the natural law (*lex naturae*) doctrines of the Middle Ages. Tro-eltsch,[2] and Max Weber before him, contended that Luther here as elsewhere allowed natural law to have a determining influence on his views, and moreover, that the Reformation participated in an important way in the further development of this concept. However, this introduces something into Luther's world of thought that is completely alien and only distorts it.

For the writers named above, the concept *lex naturae* holds a dual meaning. First, the unalterable conditions of the external aspects of nature in general as well as of man's nature. However, Luther referred to this concept only inasmuch as he considered the evil instinct as ingrained and ineradicable in a part of humanity (but only a part; in the others nature is changed by God). Yet, Luther does not attempt to justify the right and duty of the state merely on the basis of its function to suppress evil. Only Troeltsch believes Luther to have thought so crudely as to consider punishment and restrictions values in themselves. The real Luther justifies the right of the state not by its negative aspects, but by its positive ones, such as the education toward justice and the spirit of community to which the state exposes its citizens, thereby supporting the kingdom of God and even helping in its realization. Even for the constantly striving Christian such education can be of great value. Secondly—and this comes closer to the historical approach— for these writers natural law is founded on original nature as manifested in the original equality of men and the original world community. It is thus the true law, in contrast to the artificial creation of civilization. Yet, Luther, in fact, totally rejected the natural law concept. Even the thought that any natural endowment should carry a right with it runs completely counter to his ideas. Therefore, he ignores or rejects such concepts, developed during the Middle Ages, as the birth rights of man, people's sovereignty, contracts of rulers, and similar things. Nor was the situation in this respect different with Melanchthon, who was admittedly more enamored of natural law. Melanchthon explicitly pronounces as insufficient the doctrine that derives the state indirectly from God and directly from divinely given reason.[3] Similarly he rejects Occam's statement that the power of the ruler rests on the assent of the people.[4] The rights of government are rather determined by the Fourth Commandment. The truth is, therefore, exactly the opposite of what Troeltsch and Weber contend: The Reformation everywhere plays down natural law and replaces the proofs derived therefrom with arguments that are taken from Christian morality.

For just this reason, because Luther derives the state, not from below, but exclusively from above, from God's plan of salvation, he insists on its distinct character as a state whose essence is authority (*Obrigkeitsstaat*). This is the meaning of including one's duty to the government in the Fourth Commandment. Consequently the subject has no right of revolution whatsoever. Not even when the magistrate rules "according to agreed upon articles" and is guilty of a breach of his oath. Even in this instance Luther raises the objection against revolution, that the rebel wishes to be a judge in his own case, which seems to him a patent contradiction. Accordingly Luther also desires that the government hold its position with power. He complains bitterly about the lax discipline that prevailed at his time both in the Empire and in the individual states.[5] But if he demands order in the state and emphatically calls upon governments to use their power to this end, he does not mean that force is sufficient in itself. He did not idly characterize the state as "the highest work of reason." "Reason" must always be present in the use of force. That a rule which is borne with aversion, resentment, and enmity cannot endure,[6] that it is evil if a people does not love its ruler but can only fear him,[7] that force without reason cannot last at all [8]—these are truths that he constantly emphasized. Even a purely absolutist state, in which there are no lower "magistrates," but only officials who are agents of the sovereign, seemed to him something unendurable, tyrannical.[9]

His concern for the "reasonable" and thus the influence of Christian morality are even more clearly apparent in the manner in which Luther determines the duty of the state. In this context he indeed generally uses the very modest sounding formula that the state is responsible for the "physical welfare" of its subjects. But in reality he extends the meaning of "physical" quite considerably. He includes in it that the state establishes schools, that in order to prevent unchastity it encourages early marriage, that it fosters music and the arts, so that ultimately the whole realm of culture falls under this concept. Melanchthon nailed down this concept in his own way when he coined the slogan that the custody of both tables of the law is entrusted to the government.

In summary, in Lutheran territories the Reformation helped that view triumph which saw in the state something superior to the individual will, an institution which served to direct all the efforts of the people; at the same time the Reformation gave the decisive impetus to the development of the constitutional state into a cultural community (*Kulturstaat*).

But at the same time it was the Reformation that first set a rigid limit to the absolute power of the state. Luther also established freedom of conscience, whose defense he made an individual obligation, as a rational principle for the state. The means that the state utilizes and must utilize are at the same time the limits of its power. By the coercive power to the use of which it is entitled it can subjugate the body; but it cannot reach the soul; if the state attempts this, it will only produce hypocrites.

This basic principle of Luther was taken up by his followers. It was observed at the very first opportunity that offered itself, the visita-

tion in the Electorate of Saxony in 1527-8. On
this occasion the Elector of Saxony explicitly
renounced the forcible coercion of any subjects to his faith. It was not his intention, so
the instructions read, to bind anyone as to what
he should hold or believe. Therefore, the
Elector allowed those who dissented the freedom to leave the country. This occurrence in a
small German territory had general historical
significance. It was a departure from a tradition
of more than a thousand years, the first fundamental limitation of its own powers by the
state and a first formal recognition of individual right in matters of faith.

The implication of this event is not lessened
by the fact that the state's concession had
certain limits, i.e., that the ruler required dis-
senters to emigrate and that even the evangelical state permitted a law on heresy to continue to a certain extent. With respect to the
first the authorities did not lack a sense of the
harshness of the action—which, incidentally,
did not turn out to be practical in Saxony. The
Elector, however, insisted that otherwise "disorder and all kinds of injustice" would occur
in his territory. He was under the impression
that it was impossible to rule a country with
two confessions, an assumption that appears
understandable in view of the custom established by many centuries. But a historical view

must in this instance place the emphasis on the permission to emigrate, not the compulsion. For this constitutes progress, whose magnitude becomes very clear with the denial of this right to the Huguenots by Louis XIV. Particularly since in Saxony departure might take place honorably. The evangelical state on its part passes no judgment on the faith of the emigrant. Neither at that time, nor at any time whatsoever, did the Protestant states brand a Catholic a "heretic" for his faith, let alone punish him.[10] He could even stay in the country, if he kept quiet. The law on heresy, which the evangelical states still held necessary, pertained only to those who questioned the doctrine of the Trinity and of the divinity of Christ, i.e., not to those who deviated from the specific evangelical doctrine, but to those who denied a basic and universal Christian doctrine, a doctrine whose truth seemed so certain that to touch it must count as indubitable blasphemy. And even in this instance the Protestant law on heresy goes into effect, in contrast to the Catholic, only when someone speaks publicly against these doctrines.[11]

One will, therefore, have to concede to the Reformation respect, which only a prejudiced or superficial writing of history could have denied, for being the first of all in modern times to have prepared the way for freedom

of conscience in the state. All further victories
with respect to tolerance rest on this first step
during the Saxon visitation. And this holds
true despite the increasing pressure in the
Protestant countries stemming from the victory
of Melanchthon's teaching, according to which
the ruling prince must also accept responsibility
for the right religious worship. For the crucial
freedom to emigrate always remained a possibility of the last resort for those wishing,
above all, to maintain their freedom of conscience. In the Religious Peace of Augsburg
Protestantism succeeded in winning for the
Empire, i.e., for Catholic realms as well, what
had already been won in the Lutheran prov-
inces. The Peace of Westphalia set the final
seal on this. Even outside Germany it is the
Protestant countries that lead the way in tolerance. Only the recognition that they were in-
juring themselves by their intolerance finally
prompted the Catholic countries to follow this
example.[12] And neither the emergence of the
"concept of relative truth" in the period of
Enlightenment nor the emergence of reason as
against the authoritarian belief paved the way
for the still growing idea of religious liberty of
modern times. (As has already been pointed
out, reason itself could be quite intolerant, not
only in the religious but also even in its own
sphere and often still continues to be so.) What

did bring about this new religious freedom was the experience gained from the practical experiment of the states—and only the states could make such an experiment—that a fair measure of order could be maintained in a state that tolerated several religious creeds. Again, this experience was gained first and foremost in Brandenburg-Prussia and in England and America.

At least from the Protestant point of view it is impossible to regret the rigors that forced emigration originally brought with it. They were a test of character and in their effects brought glory to Protestantism. The large numbers who regularly left the country under forced re-Catholicization, the hundreds of pastors who sacrificed their offices, are proof of how deeply Luther's earnestness of conscience had gripped his followers. Nowhere do any Catholic counterexamples exist. Even the Enlightenment does not compare to advantage with orthodoxy here. If, to name only a few, one compares Flacius, who allowed himself to be driven out again and again rather than give up his convictions, or Paul Gerhardt with the corresponding behavior of a Lessing, a Semler, a Kant, or a Rousseau, one sees that the progress to a "relative" point of view, which the Enlightenment brought, had its painful obverse side.

But, even leaving religious convictions aside, Luther did not in the least intend that the subject, because he should not cause disorder, was obligated to recognize every edict of the government forthwith as just and good.[13] He himself never failed to speak plainly when something appeared wrong to him, and the Gnesio-Lutherans exerted themselves to imitate him. But the influence of Melanchthon was also at work and more effective than that of Luther. It was Melanchthon indeed who unceasingly preached to his students that a subject must yield humbly to his prince because of his limited understanding of politics. The subject has the duty to believe in the higher wisdom of rulers because he himself is not able to comprehend affairs and because the *status quo* is always better than it appears, particularly as it appears to impetuous youth.[14]

This factual advantage over Luther that Melanchthon enjoyed comes to light at another point with even more far-reaching significance. Troeltsch censured the Reformation because it did not give any impetus to the formation of a body of laws of its own. This verdict cannot include Luther. He had a highly gifted insight into the spirit of a particular body of law, for the advantages and disadvantages of the Roman, Germanic, and Mosaic law;[15] more clearly than any contemporary he noted that all law was conditioned by a particular ethos and he still desired even in his last days to make a boisterous sally into the midst of the jurists. But what Troeltsch overlooked was that the period of the Reformation coincided with another period in which an already complete large-scale system of law was pressing forward victoriously in Germany. Luther did not allow the Roman law to blind him. He did not reject it, nor did he find it to be the best. Melanchthon was of another mind. The latter valued Roman law, simply because of its antiquity, with the unreserved enthusiasm that the humanists were wont to display in fields where they were not experts. Roman law is so full of moderation and humanity—Luther had felt the lack precisely of truly humane consideration in Roman law as compared with the Mosaic—that the Germans could only congratulate themselves on it.[16] Every question that moves in the no man's land between law and morality is already decided for Melanchthon by the fact that Roman law provides a definite solution, even the question of whether the peasant may hunt in the woods. In this instance one can see with particular clarity that the union of Reformation and humanism was not always advantageous. It also had this effect, that the impetus for a further development of law which could have arisen from the Lutheran conception of morality was strangled at birth and at the same time "subjects" were encouraged to surrender their own judgments in legal and political questions.

The actual consequence was that in the Lutheran states the government occupied the sole decision-making position. The Reformation did not hinder, but rather encouraged the growth of absolutism in Germany.[17] What Luther said about the necessity of lower magistrates and Melanchthon about the value of "ephors" (cf. below) ultimately had only the effect that the memory of the concept of the rights of the estates never disappeared completely from political theory. A fair historical judgment must nevertheless recognize that Luther did not in vain seriously admonish the consciences of the nobility with respect to their duties. Not only Frederick the Great demonstrated the truth of the statement, which is completely in the spirit of Luther,[18] that the ruler was the first servant of the state. Among subjects the conviction of the ethical worth of the state produced a commitment to the whole which was prepared even for heavy sacrifices. The inner resources of the state were thus greatly increased. Herein lies the reason why the Protestant lands recovered so quickly from the Thirty Years' War, why small, thinly populated Sweden played a European role for a time, and why poor Prussia could become a great power.

In international affairs, on the other hand, Luther's ideas from the beginning had a crippling rather than a strengthening effect. Luther drew the consequences of his concept of community and his interpretation of the love commandment for diplomacy as well. He will tolerate war at best only as defensive war and obligates not only the individual but also the state upon occasion to accept unjust treatment passively. He thereby encourages the state not only to resign its natural aspirations for expansion but also to suppress that sense of honor which is so important for the state and for national consciousness. And though he had some understanding for war and its manliness, whenever it was unavoidable, he lacked all comprehension of politics and the utilization of the opportune moment as well as the calculated intrigues of diplomacy. He always consoled himself with the thought that things were not as bad as all that and that last-minute changes for the better might yet occur. His politically gifted supporters, like Philip of Hesse and Butzer, were never able to make Luther change his views on this. In the same vein, Melanchthon branded the striving for a "universal monarchy" as an ungodly enterprise.[19] And all this at a time when politics purely for the "interest" of the state is developed into an art, when the "reputation" of the state gains tremendously in meaning, and when out of powerful battles between Hapsburg, Spain, and France the concept of "monarchy," replacing the old emperor-ideal, emerges in new form.[20] Despite all this, Lutheranism remained in Luther's tracks. One may well attribute it to the influence of his spirit that from its soil grew many able administrators but few outstanding politicians; and even the few that could qualify as such are distinctly influenced by the Lutheran attitude. One need only recall the role that the question of the justification of "monarchy" (always meaning "universal monarchy") played in the thinking of Gustavus Adolphus and his catchword about the "affected dominion" of the Emperor, which must collapse of its own weight like the fourth world-empire of the prophet Daniel. Consequently in Lutheran territories one could find an innumerable crowd of excellent administrators, but very few statesmen in the grand style. As soon as it arose, the principle of *raison d'état* encountered strong opposition. Even Frederick the Great felt it necessary to write his *"Antimachiavell."* And one need only compare Bismarck with Cromwell to recognize the Lutheran character of his statecraft. Bismarck was the avowed enemy of preventive war. He never presumed to wage war as an instrument of justice;[21] when, as was his duty, he thought to make Germany into a state capable of surviving —this is his presumed "power politics"—he, at the same time, not only at the conclusion of peace but also as part of his diplomacy, took into consideration what was necessary to the survival of other nations.[22] Finally, as a consequence of this Lutheran disposition the German people never had an instinct favorable to expansionist politics. Imperialism in the sense of dominion in the world or even a solitary dominion could never possess the German people. This would have been that "universal monarchy" which one dreaded. Great successes in the realm of foreign affairs regularly led to an anxious fear—quite in the spirit of Luther, but totally unintelligible for an Englishman— that external success had been bought at the peril of the soul. The [First] World War has made this shatteringly apparent. It was only necessary to persuade the German people that it was no longer fighting a defensive war but a war of conquest, and its power vanished.

In Calvinism the Reformation ideas influenced the concept of the state in the opposite direction.

There the question of armed resistance to government, which had only transient significance for Lutheranism and ultimately played only an academic role, became an issue of fundamental importance.

Luther roundly denied this right to the individual and even in the relation of lower to higher magistrates,[23] i.e., of the nobles to the Emperor, he took the possibility of its affirmation into consideration only when weighty reasons were presented to him out of positive law. He did not want to hear anything about "natural law" proofs. Even at this point the fact is verified that the Reformation consciously underemphasized natural law. Even though the Reformation actually represents a turning point, its representatives, particularly Luther —quite in contrast to the Enlightenment—are filled with a deep respect for what has developed in the process of time, because this, as it has developed, did not come about without the will of God. If they had to go beyond it, they strove, as far as possible, to maintain continuity with the existing situation. In our particular concern Luther drew the consequence, when he gave in to the constitutional arguments—the responsibility for their validity he placed on the jurists—that at best one is permitted to resist, but not required. It always seemed to him a more Christian course of action for the nobility to surrender their rights and to submit the matter to God in patient obedience. This disposition continued to burden the German Protestants when out of necessity they resolved on real resistance. They conducted neither the Smalkald War nor the Thirty Years' War with the decisiveness the situation required. No one thought at all to use the right of resistance of the estates, which on this occasion was strengthened by use, later on as a weapon against growing absolutism. Melanchthon indeed coined scientific terms[24] that served as beginnings, also found in German legal thought, which political theory developed further into a doctrine of universal human rights, but in practice this remained completely without significance in Germany.

The temper of Calvinism[25] was different from the beginning. Calvin indeed leans very closely on Luther in his political theory, too;[26] in the particular point at issue he therefore shares Luther's position that only historical law, not natural law, is relevant. But just as in all areas he enlarges the participation of Christians in the state—he fought the opinion that the state was only a necessary evil and therefore gives the Christian without qualification the right to undertake litigation—so also in this point he goes beyond Luther. If estates are present in a people, indeed only when such estates are present—for Calvin is no more desirous of hearing of a "popular" right of revolution than Luther—these estates have not merely a right, but indeed the duty to oppose the unjust actions of a government. In the strongest language Calvin lays this duty upon the conscience of those appointed to these offices. As early as the *Institutes* of 1536 he writes that it would be criminal faithlessness, a betrayal of a divinely entrusted custody of popular freedom, if the estates evaded this duty.[27] In the second edition of 1539, revised in Strasbourg, he adds a similar sentence about urban magistrates.[28] Behind the admonition there appears in Calvin the figure of an "avenger," whom God could awaken to liberate an enslaved people if those called were remiss in their duty. Luther had already occasionally touched on something similar in alluding to the appearance of the Old Testament judges, but he made the idea immediately impractical, for who today would presume to feel himself, like Samson, to be called of God? Calvin, too, warns emphatically against the possibility that someone will consider himself this "avenger" because the role pleases him. But in the context in which he expresses his thought the allusion to the possibility nevertheless takes on significance as a kind of warning.[29]

The pressure of an unbearable external situation forced Calvinism beyond the limits set by Calvin. Everywhere, indeed, in the Netherlands as in Scotland and France, Calvin's followers began the fight for their faith, quite in Calvin's sense, with the watchword that it was at the same time necessary to defend the traditional freedom of the estates. But when it became a life-and-death struggle, it became clear that this position did not suffice. For nowhere had the estates as such chosen Calvinism decisively. If Calvinism did not want to surrender itself, it had to go one step further. Under the impact of St. Bartholomew's night the Monarchomachs in France dared to do this and reached back beyond the positive law, which had always been their initial starting point, to natural law. They did so hesitantly, with careful weighing of the reasons. Only in an extreme situation, when the nobility not only fails, but itself participates in tyranny, may "the people," according to Du Plessis-Mornay, have the right of resistance. John Knox in Scotland had earlier come to the same conclusion with similar degrees of qualification. Calvinism thus gained the opportunity to rally the masses and to pursue their battle in this way. But what was born under the pressure of necessity always remained in practice only an auxiliary means over against the original idea. The goal was nowhere the establishment of popular sovereignty, but only of securing the rights of the estates in addition to winning religious freedom. In England and the Low

Countries Calvinism actually achieved this goal.
In this way Calvinism, on its part, placed a solid
barrier in the path of the spread of absolutism
in Europe. Moreover, one is justified in giving
more credit for the final success to the religious
impulses, i.e., to the Reformation, than to the
purely political movement associated with it.
For without the impetuous power with which
Calvinism, and only Calvinism, could endow the
resistance, parliamentary government would
have gone under not only in the Low Countries,
but also in the England of the Stuarts, as it
did in the rest of Europe.

Something more, however, developed out of
the struggles in England,[30] something pointed
at the individual. The new phenomenon is,
first of all, conditioned by the peculiar development that the religious ideas of Calvinism
underwent in England.

The distortion in the relation between individual and community, referred to briefly on
page 41 above, is already seen in its incipient
stage in Puritanism. In contrast to Continental
Calvinism. Puritanism did not achieve an
orderly ecclesiastical constitution. This was not
without its effects on the religious self-consciousness of its followers. The individual here
lacks the strong, even religious support, which
in pure Calvinism he found in the community.
To a greater degree he feels that he stands

alone and that he has to seek in himself the power for inner renewal. Thus the personal experience of conversion, the identification marks and the personal verification of Christian status in a perfect life receive here a much greater weight than was the case elsewhere in Protestantism. This individualization of the believer even increases, moreover, in the smaller communities that came out of Puritanism, the Independents, Baptists, Seekers, Quakers, and all the others. In these, under the influence in part of liberal ideas, in part of enthusiastic-mystic ideas, the early Reformation concept disappears, namely, that it was possible to bring just about everybody to religious certainty within a specific universally valid form. God himself converts the individual and He follows His own particular ways of doing things with each one; one must wait until the hour comes and dare not by clumsy interference disturb the spiritual growth of another. Accordingly, the individual enters the community after he has been converted; he does not experience conversion within the community. The introduction of the baptism of adults by the Baptists was only an affirmation of a basic concept, independently arrived at in England.

The emphasis on this religious individualism resulted in passionate opposition to the state church, which would coerce the individual with its "uniformity" and defraud him of his greatest treasure, his personal experience of God. But from this very emphasis there followed a demand for tolerance in a new sense. The position is now attained in which tolerance is demanded, not because of indifference to religion, but for the sake of religion. And indeed not as tolerance only for a community or a group, but—this at least was the final consequence—for every individual.

But in England the conditions were—in contrast to those on the Continent—favorable for the political manifestations of religious principles. Butzer, whose writings strongly influenced Puritanism, derived in his *De Regno Christi* very specific suggestions for reforms for the state and the community from the religious concept of the kingdom of God. At this point of the religious development of the various sects another, peculiarly Anglo-Saxon trait became noticeable. The mysticism which these sects practiced did not alienate them from the world nor from their people; it did not even alienate them from their national self-consciousness. Their representatives all remain self-consciously Englishmen, who are proud of their England and their English birth. Nothing so clearly reveals the power attained by the national enthusiasm which at that time seized the individual Englishman than that it should be able to assert itself alongside of and within a mysticism that otherwise obliterated all distinctions. Indeed, in these sects one is more likely to find, along with religious self-consciousness, a heightening of national self-consciousness. A few among them, the Diggers and the Fifth Monarchists, even emphasize the purely Anglo-Saxon in contrast to that brought in through alien rule, through the Norman Conquest. Consequently the majority of their followers had no desire to emigrate permanently into any foreign country—one should not forget that the American colonies were at that time English and that the emigrants to these parts continued to feel themselves Englishmen—they want to stay at home, they insist on their right, which is theirs by birth, to live in just this country and to move about it undisturbed.

Under these quite peculiar historical conditions the demands for religious and civic freedom with respect to the individual could be fused so that henceforth religious freedom appeared as the essence of civic freedom or, contrariwise, civic freedom as the necessary fulfillment of the religious freedom. The consequence was, as Jellinek has shown, that the concept of universal human right, bringing together both religious and civic ideas, first expressed in the charters of individual North

American colonies and in the Bill of Rights, achieved world significance through the constitution of the United States and the French Revolution.

This was a development that went beyond what the Reformers desired. For, just like Luther, Calvin absolutely rejected the possibility of deriving consequences for political life from religious freedom.[31] Nevertheless, after Jellinek's demonstration it should never again have been contested that the power that gave the actual impetus and forced matters to a conclusion was the religious feeling arising from the Reformation. True, the idea of universal human rights can be traced back even to the Middle Ages; but its formal acceptance into political theory is not completed until this period and only under the impact of religion. For at that time in England as in America religious freedom occupied the foreground. In addition, freedom of religion was something clear and plainly defined, so that one knew what one was fighting for and could unite in subscribing to it; meanwhile, the related "human" and "natural rights" were always conditioned in content by the momentary economic situation and the particular wishes of individual social classes. That religious rights set the pace is always revealed by the bounds within which the human rights that were achieved were held.

The socialistic demands of the Levellers, Fifth Monarchists, and Diggers foundered. Not because they were "utopian": for much of what the Levellers desired was later realized; but because no convincing religious power was associated with them. For the religious thought that developed in the sects focused only on the individual. It could thus effectively support only that which had reference to the individual. There is justification in the social-democratic verdict that sees in universal human rights only the realization of the demands of the bourgeoisie. As they were proclaimed then and even in the French Revolution, they were sufficient and a source of pride only for the person who was able to stand as a self-sufficient individual economically or who was able to help himself get ahead. The masses of the have-nots were not benefited.

The acceptance of universal human rights into the constitution was, however, not just the modification of a single point; it included in itself the transformation of the whole concept of the state. This is most apparent in America, where human rights became the starting point for the concept of the state. There the individual with his inalienable rights stands first. Only beyond this boundary does the right of the state begin. The state takes its place in a purposive association which governs those matters that are indispensable for the common life. But even in England, where universal human rights were looked upon as only the minimum amount of rights which the individual could lay claim to within the state, they worked in the same unsettling manner. The remarkable fact confronts one that the same Reformation ideas that in Germany developed feeling for the state and drew only the sharp boundary of freedom of conscience for the power of the state, in another place, as a result of the concept of personality, helped to transform the state into a mere framework.

Still in England this dissolution encounters a force for unity which in its origin also is related to the Reformation. Since the dissolution of the tie with Rome and the establishment of the Church of England one encounters in England a peculiar, religiously colored self-awareness, which is related to the English people as such. It is derived from the state church and not, as is commonly believed, from Puritanism—for how could a minority, especially a minority in the position of conflict, have influenced the general national consciousness?[32] As accidentally as it arose and as planlessly as it was built—already to some extent under Edward VI and completely under Elizabeth—this church became the object of a great pride. One rarely sees clearly on the Continent what it means for the self-consciousness of Englishmen that it was not as in Germany a minor elector or duke, but an actual king, a sovereign ruler, who as a "new Josiah" stepped to the head of the Reformation, and that not just a "population," but an entire people rallied around him. As early as under Edward VI this situation gives rise to the belief in a special religious blessing of the English people. It crystallizes into the consciousness of an elect people and in this intensification it carries all Englishmen along with it. It lives in the Puritans and sectarians no less than in the members of the state church. As early as Cromwell this religious national feeling, which replaced the feeling for the state, becomes the driving force of English imperialism. For England did not have the Lutheran aversion to "universal monarchy," much less the fear that external success might lead to *hybris*. Every further extension of the British Empire served rather to strengthen the conviction that along with it the kingdom of God was also growing. This religiously grounded imperialistic drive could even make use of the "liberal" thought that at times obstructed it. If England was the refuge of freedom and humanity, then she also possessed the moral right constantly to extend her power, which was at the same time the bearer of humanity.

This national self-consciousness provides the foundation for the English conception of war. E. Hirsch has strikingly demonstrated that England has in a special way appropriated the teachings of Hugo Grotius that war may be conceived as an undertaking for justice and punishment. This provides the person who trusts himself to play the role of a judge of nations with the advantage that the difficult question of offensive or defensive war is excluded from the beginning. For in the name of the sanctity of justice war can be undertaken at any time even against a nation that has "injured," not the English people, but a third country. But there follows, in addition, the necessity of treating the conquered as a criminal whom she burdens not only with complete reparation, but also keeps under observation until his eventual "reform" takes place. England always and above all in the [First] World War acted on this principle. What Germany would have considered insufferable self-righteousness, what Bismarck, the purest representative of German thought in this matter, firmly rejected, Englishmen on the basis of this religious self-appraisal practiced with the best of conscience.[33]

Similar tensions and contradictions could also arise in the economic sphere out of the motiva-

tions interrelated by Luther. By proclaiming
the duty to work for the sake of production and
by proclaiming simultaneously the spirit of
humble simplicity, Luther gave a tremendous
boost to the economic production of goods. But
at the same time, following his concept of
community, Luther emphasizes not only the individual's duty of consideration and helpful-
ness toward his neighbor but also the duty of
the community as a whole to take care of those
unable to work and to protect the weak from
the strong. The important thing was how the
two concepts developed in relation to each
other.

For the first concept it was of primary importance that Luther and the reformers in
general founded their recognition of private
property on their over-all appreciation for
work. True, Luther declared that in principle
it should be a matter of indifference to the
Christian whether the wages of his work are
paid to him personally or to a collective community fund. But Luther did not recognize a
duty toward communism as it was conceived
by the Anabaptists, not even if one were to
refer to Adam or an archetypal community.
All the more so, since he knew from his experience in the monastery that even communism
could not do away completely with private
property and that, furthermore, the realization

of communism was founded on the exploitation of the capable and industrious by the lazy. It seemed to him that the Christian command to love, which the Anabaptists claimed as their banner, actually confirmed the idea of private property. For whoever wants to give unto others must first have something to give.

But when Luther demanded work, it is clear that he meant altogether honest work and this alone forced him to take a stand on the then dominating forms of business enterprise.

It was decisive for his conception of the problem that he lived in a state in which agriculture was still dominant and the newly expanding capitalism just beginning to exhibit its effects. Luther sees the bad side of capitalism. He observed—and thus he proves himself a good observer of his time—the brutalization of mercantile ethics, "the fast and evil artifices" now practiced, the monopolies, the cartels, the option business, the sham transactions, the fraudulent bankruptcy, and the careless handling of credit. He also observed the evil consequences of foreign trade for popular morals in the increase of luxury and the rise of new and foolish necessities.

Influenced by such impressions, Luther first of all intervened strongly for the meaning and moral value of agriculture. Over against industry and trade, agriculture seemed to him the most natural activity. "I do not see," he wrote, "many good customs which have ever come into a country through commerce. This is why God in former times let his people of Israel live by the sea and not engage in commerce. . . . This I know well, that it is much more godly to till the land than to engage in commerce and those do better who follow the Scriptures in exploiting the soil and seeking their nourishment from it. . . . Much land is still unexploited and unsowed." At least in respect to doctrine, he thereby in no way merely set forth the self-evident, which had already secured the protection of tradition for itself. For one must remember that the moral teaching of the scholastics, particularly of St. Thomas, at all points prefers the city dweller. The peasant is regularly forgotten by it or appears as the contemptible appendage of the wealthy urban population. It was Luther's deed that he again brought honor to the peasant, and if one holds that his position in the Peasants' War must be condemned, then in all fairness his intervention on behalf of the peasant's work should be thrown into the scale as a counterweight. More than Luther's present-day accusers, the peasantry itself seems to have sensed his support. For it is hardly an accident that the Reformation became so deeply rooted in this particular estate.

On the other hand, Luther sharply attacked the growing money economy. Not only its excesses, which, as he thought, condemned themselves, but also those forms that at the time were found unobjectionable or even tolerable. He attacks with new arguments, born from the depths of his own understanding, the form of finance most widespread at the time, usury. What was objectionable to him in the first place was not that the usurer usually exploited another's need, but just the fact that he collected his safe interest "without either effort or risk." This contradicted his principle of the duty to work. And when in addition usury was handled as a "blind" sale, i.e., money was lent on credit alone, it appeared to him to be a piece of charlatanry which must corrupt both parties. Luther had the courage to set up the demands of the Sermon on the Mount as a serious reform program for the current practices. The principle found there, to lend money without interest or where possible to give it to the needy, he preserves as a strict Christian obligation, in so far as one person has a surplus and the other is not averse to work. Luther thought that this alone, seriously practiced, would go far in bringing about a healthier situation. For the greatest part of the existing usurious agreements would thereby decline. However, in so far as the condition that one party has a surplus is not met and therefore, with consideration for both parties, the agreement on interest is indispensable, in fact appears useful, Luther would at least ennoble its practice in a Christian sense. Above all, "blind" money lending must be done away with. If one returns to sound business practices, in which money is lent only on specified commodities, it is possible to make the payment of interest conform to reason and charity. Since the commodity in question is always profit-producing, the interest can be kept in line with the actual income (assuming the industry of the debtor). In any case, four or at most six per cent per year must be the limit.

Luther also had his own opinions about the setting of prices in retail trade. He sought a new way to determine the "just price," so that the application of labor became its base; in addition, the various kinds of labor were to be equitably recognized and for the calculation of the exchange value of labor the wage of the ordinary day laborer was to be taken as the lower limit.

It is incomprehensible that in the face of such decisive proposals on the part of Luther one can accuse him of "capitulating to the autonomy of economic life" and actually setting aside the commandments of the Sermon on the Mount. If at any place, then surely at this,

Luther fought for obedience to Christian principles in the Christian life. But at this point, too, Melanchthon comes between him and the next generation.[34] Melanchthon never felt the tension between the Sermon on the Mount and business practices as sharply as Luther did. In the economics of finance he indeed shares with Luther the view of the unproductiveness of money—how could he doubt it, since the principle came from Aristotle—and he condemns taking interest on unsecured loans as usury. Contrary to Luther, however, who constantly saw through the deception, he declared return sales and the taking of interest with security to be true sales; this implied, therefore, that the money when returned, i.e., including the interest, was not usurious. And the unsecured loan, which Luther had condemned root and branch, he defended on no less than four grounds, even with the help of canon law, and he also had nothing against the interest, which Luther opposed. For the entire problem he sets up the rule that the Christian may utilize such forms of business which the laws, i.e., above all Roman law, approved and declared to be respectable.[35] This meant as much as a surrender of any control according to Christian principles.

The position of Lutheranism on this question was therefore not unified. On the whole the comfortable views of Melanchthon triumphed. Consequently, Lutheranism participated with a quiet conscience in the economy as it was developing; indeed North German Protestant governments were among the first to give up the campaign against the taking of interest as such; to be sure, they did so to counteract secret usury more successfully. Despite this, something of Luther's attitude reawakened in Pietism. Pietism took industry in one's calling, including business, as a serious Christian duty and thus arrived at an entrepreneurial drive that was occasionally far-reaching; but in addition it considered it a fixed principle that the degree of profit must also correspond to the contribution to the kingdom of God.

Calvin found himself in a different situation from Luther. He lived in a community that had at its disposal only a very small territory, which could not provide the city with an adequate food supply and in which, in addition, trade and industry had received a mortal blow from French economic policy. Therefore, Calvin had little occasion to think about the significance of agriculture, but more reason to reflect on the significance of commerce and industry. If Geneva was to be helped to its feet at all, it could only be by the revival of these two branches of activity. Yet, Calvin never intended to turn Geneva into a city like Venice. For, above all the urgencies of external demands, he did not forget his New Testament.[36]

He did indeed take an important step in the direction of finance by breaking with the Aristotelian view that money was sterile.[37] Not in vain was he a jurist of a scholarly and independent mind, who did not allow respect for Aristotle to blind him. He also had enough insight into the reality of things to recognize that interest had an inherent justification, for without it no commerce whatsoever was possible.[38] In addition, however, Calvin felt himself as strictly bound as Luther to the Sermon on the Mount and his knowledge of business allowed him to see through the deceptions that were possible in this area even more sharply than the German Reformers. He not only knew just as well as Luther that the word "interest" is capable of unlimited extension; in contrast to Melanchthon, he also comprehended that within the most beautiful legal forms one can practice the worst usury. Consequently his remarks on particular instances are essentially closer to Luther than to Melanchthon. Above all, he considers the occupation of money lending for the purpose of profit as incompatible with Christianity, and consequently also, as he stated expressly, the management of a bank. For the banker appeared to him as someone who, himself idle, wants to make a profit without working for it, and to top it off, in many cases exploits persons in need. This appeared to him to be a clear case of usury.[39] Calvin set the banker along with every other Christian under the strict rule of Matt. 7:12. A Christian may not desire to become rich at the expense of another; love must also rule in such affairs.[40] And Calvin understands this rule in the same sense that Luther did, namely, that interest may be taken only from those with possessions;[41] to take it from the poor is unjust. Especially where necessity is evident, the obligation becomes binding on everyone who is able to act according to the Sermon on the Mount.[42] In the same manner Calvin makes clear that even in justified and unavoidable financial transactions one must not think that one must always charge five per cent because this is permitted by the authorities.[43]

There can be no justification, therefore, for the opinion that Calvin allowed his church to run full sail into the money economy. He put more difficult obstacles in its way than the Lutheranism that Melanchthon led.

Calvin himself, when he considered everything, had had the feeling that the charging of interest was at best a most dubious affair for the Christian: some form of taking advantage of one's neighbor was always part of it.

From the directives issued by Calvin his church later derived a definite doctrine. This doctrine is uniformly taught by Viret, Danäus, Rivetus, Gisbert Voëtius, Perkins, and Amesius and is thus as valid in the Netherlands and among the Puritans in England as it is in France and Geneva.[44] It holds with Calvin that no interest at all may be asked from the needy, but that it is rather the duty of the Christian to support him with interest-free loans or gifts. In monetary transactions with the wealthy, involving interest rates, these are justified by regarding them as the due gratitude toward the lender or as the fair share of profit accruing from the particular transaction. But it is also necessary to draw the consequences from this view, namely that if the borrowed loses the capital, or the profit, without his fault, the money lender can not claim interest nor even the immediate repayment of his capital. It should also be stressed that, of all places, in England a movement developed which, going beyond Calvin straight back to Luther, favored the complete outlawing of all interest rates. Butzer combated this view. Nevertheless, Edward VI, probably on the advice of Latimer, prohibited the charging of interest by a law in 1551 and 1552. And even after Elizabeth in 1571 had again permitted interests of up to ten per cent—James I reduced them to eight per cent—Puritanism continued to hold not only to the Calvinist but even to the still more severe Lutheran doctrine. The latter had able supporters even among bishops, such as Jewel, Pilkington, Sandys, and as late as the beginning of the seventeenth century, Lancelot Andrewes.

All this existed not only on paper[45] in the Calvinist churches. All the means at the disposal of the Calvinist church discipline were put to work to enforce it. In France the banker was declared unworthy of the position of presbyter. Serious arguments arose even over the issue of whether the church may at least invest the money allocated for the care of the poor with interest. In the Netherlands the approach was even more radical. There, the "Lombards" (money lenders) as well as their families and employees were mercilessly excluded from communion and the church did not even accept donations from them. Even in England Jewel dared denounce usurers by name during church service and threatened their expulsion from the church.

Thus, here too, the situation was just the reverse of what it is usually assumed to have been. No church has ever attempted to emulate the word of the Lord in the Sermon on the Mount so completely as the Calvinist church till the middle of the seventeenth century. Therefore, no church has fought "capitalism" as persistently as the Calvinist church.[46] Not until Hugo Grotius and Salmasius did anyone attempt to modify this rigorousness, and even they did not do it simply by recalling the law of nature—at least not Troeltsch's concept of it, which considers the inevitability of a thing sufficient justification for it. What both did was first to explain interest rates on the basis of their importance in business life and then to justify them also morally. First, on the basis of natural morality (which is actually their right-of-nature concept): interest is, so they reasoned in Calvinistic tradition, due gratitude for assistance rendered. Next, on the basis of Christianity: here their justification is that the commandment of the Sermon on the Mount was really a "super-commandment" intended only for the perfect.

At first a storm of indignation arose in the Netherlands against this actual disregard for the Sermon on the Mount and against the disrespect for the profound difference in principle between lending money to the needy and to the wealthy. The main target of the protest became Salmasius, the "shield bearer of the Lombards."

But the spirit of the times was stronger than the force of the Calvinist church. The barbarism brought about by the big wars and the simultaneous growth of business and commercial interests has prevented Calvinism since the middle of the seventeenth century from upholding its discipline. A tragic development took place: just those civil virtues to which Calvinism had educated its members—orderliness, professional pride, self-discipline, thrift, and self-denial [47]—produced in some extreme cases a kind of business enterprise which is not unjustifiably called a model for contemporary capitalism. Max Weber's famous proposition[48]—developed with questionable one-sidedness—about the rise of the spirit of capitalism out of the spirit of Calvinism, appears to me to be demonstrated by him in its essentials.[49] I would only emphasize even more strongly than he did that it was not pure Calvinism but Puritanism that took this direction, and that even in it the "capitalistic striving" unfolded itself fully only on the colonial soil of America. Here we have the exact counterpart in the sphere of economics to what we have just stated about the field of politics. Within those sects influenced by mysticism there emerges a refined religious selfishness,[50] a self-centeredness, an unrest caused by the striving for perfection, all of which overshadows the concern for the neighbor. The individual becomes preoccupied with himself and begins to look down upon others. This carries over into business dealings. It is signifi-

cant that none of the platforms of Congrega-
tionalism touch upon the issue of interest taking. But even Bunyan and George Fox wrote
nothing about it. It is thus precisely the sects
that cast aside the Sermon on the Mount on
this point. In addition, there was the pressure
from external circumstances, the exclusion from
government jobs which forced the nonconform-
ist into private business, as well as the ever
present contrast to the state church and the
"entertainments" that it sponsored. Thus, already in England the Lutheran-Calvinist values
of loyalty to a job and joyful industriousness
were transformed into that exclusive business
sense and that sober figure-mindedness which
characterized the spirit of capitalism.

However, only in America did these traits
fully unfold. To this day the American lacks
the personal relationship to the soil which is
so strongly developed with the German and
the Russian. In this respect the American always remained a colonist. He views agriculture
merely as the utilization of the soil. His entire
ability is therefore concentrated on the business
enterprise. And away from the restrictions of
the home soil which binds the individual to
national or tribal interests, the capitalistic spirit
could assert itself much more brutally than in
the Old World. Thomas Chalmers bears a
classical witness to how strangely this type of

enterprise still affected an unadulterated Calvinist at the beginning of the ninteenth century.
Chalmers identified it as something that had
just arisen, as a doctrine of "the new school,"
that one begins to reinvest one's surplus in
business and proclaims it a matter of principle
to do so, and he felt himself compelled to
oppose this doctrine both with religious and
with economic arguments. The drive for profit
for the sake of profit he cannot approve in
any way. At all events he is right in saying
that industry driven to this soul-murdering
extent directly contradicts the true purpose of
the Reformation.

At the same time it was imperative to the
reformers that the spirit of brotherhood was
not neglected in the name of individual
efficiency. For good reason they stressed this
more strongly than the duty to work, and therefore sought to create institutions to take care
of those crushed by the economic struggle or
unable to work. At the same time—keeping in
mind the first point of view—they made
certain that such action did not encourage
indolence.

Luther conceived this obligation on a mag-
nanimous scale. He liked to quote the Old
Testament passage, "There shall be no poor
among you," and thus indicated the goal that an
organized program of care for the poor must

attain and also made clear to the community its obligations to its individual members. The fact that Luther[51] also determined the place at which help should begin in a manner different from current practice meant a new step forward beyond both the existing Catholic-ecclesiastical as well as the urban care for the poor. He considers not only the lowest strata of the already completely pauperized and unemployable persons, but, as his insight into the economic situation and his evaluation of work suggested, also those members of the middle class whom poverty was just threatening or who were just struggling out of it. From this standpoint Luther defended existing social arrangements that an unthinking desire for change wished to tear down. In Erfurt he opposed the proposed weakening of the guild constitution because he saw the guilds as a protective weapon against the dominant power of capital. Completely free enterprise would, he said premonitorily, lead only to the oppression of the economically weaker. But he also gave his full support to an extension of the guild constitution in order to take care of the "dishonest" and the social climbers. And for this purpose he independently brought a new instrument into being, the "community chest," which was to work both for welfare and education. It is remarkable how strongly, even in the first draft of a relief ordinance, he insisted on the distinction between those willing to work and those who shy away from it. Succeeding ordinances, even as early as those of Wittenberg in 1522 and of Leisnig in 1523, state even more plainly that in addition to the unemployables, the so-called house poor and the artisans with little capital were to be supported by the guaranteeing of loans.

On this occasion, however, the shortcomings of the Lutheran ecclesiastical polity showed themselves. Luther thought that in the community fund government and congregation, state and church, should work together; at least in such a way that the church would give the decisive impetus.[52] But the church never instituted a separate ecclesiastical office because in this instance, too, Luther had "to wait, until the Lord God made some Christians." [53] Even elsewhere as in Hesse and Württemberg, where "deacons" were appointed, the title was no more than a name. For, in fact, the representatives of the civil community who were given administrative responsibility, although they were also to feel themselves to be agents of the church, always found purely economic considerations more to their liking than religious and ecclesiastical ones. This kind of administration made doubtful what Luther desired with respect to the spirit of this entire creation and what was expressed, for example, in the plan of Leisnig, which provided for an assembly held three times yearly in order to awaken in the total community a powerful sense of responsibility for individuals struggling with poverty. Another ground for despair arose: only as the Reformation seriously undertook to give thorough consideration to every really needy person did it become evident what powerful means were actually necessary for this work. But one could not succeed in making available on a large enough scale the ecclesiastical riches that Luther had his eye on for this purpose, the ecclesiastical fiefs, monastic possessions, and so forth. The remaining sources of income, mainly alms and offerings, did not suffice for this lofty purpose. So one had to be satisfied with something more modest, to protect at least the most destitute from starvation and destruction. The terrible privations of the Thirty Years' War and the impoverishment of the parishes forced an end even to this minimal help so that the church left this area completely vacant and the state took the obligation on itself alone. In the next one hundred and fifty years the state administered relief more frequently with police measures than in a spirit of welfare. Still there was progress in the fact that the state as such even became aware of this social obligation. The first seed for the development of the welfare state had been planted.

Its value lay not only in a more profound concept of the state as such but simultaneously —though this was felt only much later—in a protection against the narrowing down of the Christian idea of love. If the state became the administrator of public charity this served as a permanent reminder that the practice of true Christian love does not restrict itself to the members of one's own specific church, nor even to a specific segment of the population, but must be directed toward all citizens, in fact toward every human being.

Thus, if the church was to promote social progress, she was forced into the position of having to put pressure on the state, partly through suggestions and partly through the creation of new institutions. Eventually the church did just that, except that her actions did not originate with the territorial or state churches but from the followers of pietism within the church. In that connection it is significant that German Pietism was in intense contact with England, but not—I should like to emphasize—with the sects there, but with the Anglican state church. For German Pietism had a strong social awareness, which differentiates it from the English sects and demonstrates its Lutheran spirit, while England had at that time without doubt the most advanced social institutions of any country. It was from there that Spener had received his inspiration when he suggested the construction of poorhouses, workhouses, and houses of correction in the city of Frankfurt. What he had in mind was doubtlessly the English workhouse. His ideas were first carried out in Frankfurt and immediately Nuremberg, Berlin, Leipzig, Limburg, Augsburg, and Darmstadt followed suit. Later, many such houses were founded in still other German cities. The English example was also followed by utilizing these same institutions to create employment possibilities for those unable to find work. This led in many instances to the introduction of new production processes. Of course, just as in England so here too, this combination of opposite aims proved to be unworkable in the long run. A further deterioration took place as a result of the frequent placement of orphans in poor correction houses. For this reason alone Francke's orphanage in Halle signified an important step in the right direction. For in this city for the first time, at least in Germany, an orphanage was founded according to a new pattern, in so far as in the institution the customary union of orphanage, house of correction, and workhouse was broken, and thereby the viewpoint was overcome that orphans belonged among the "indolent population." Francke also succeeded in going beyond the boundaries of the church and awakening a sense of Christian charity in "educated society." For the effort of the German Enlightenment to make its concept of humanity effective also in social action can only be understood as an after-effect of Pietism. The Latin Enlightenment knows nothing of such practical ventures and in the English there were only feeble imitations. So we can credit the Reformation also with the accomplishments of the German Enlightenment. It was Pietistic circles once again who under the impact of the need created by the war at the beginning of the nineteenth century took in hand the compelling social obligations of rescuing children, combating unemployment, and ministering to prisoners. In this instance, too, an effect on the public and on the state did not fail to appear. Progress in penal administration and specifically in state and urban relief administration was achieved only under this influence. In particular the basic idea of the so-called Elberfelder system is a direct imitation of a church example.[54]

It is indeed indicative of the limits within which the social movement developing in Germany moved, that it was only Pietism which served as its carrier. The large-scale plan for a thoroughgoing reconstitution of ecclesiastical charity, which the General Synod of 1846 worked out and which at that time, remarkably, even confessional Lutheranism supported,[55] foundered on the stubbornness of Frederick William IV. Thus the opportunity was missed to make social action a matter of conscience for the church as such and at the same time to unite the numerous individual Pietistic undertakings according to a grand plan. But the Pietistic origin also brought forth an inner limitation. These circles lacked the unprejudiced eye for the social causes of the needs they combated. Even Wichern saw them ultimately only as a consequence of sin. He did not observe what the factory and the worker signified in themselves and what justified strivings arose within the working class. Thus neither church nor state succeeded in satisfying the social-democratic movement that was then growing vigorously. A just verdict on what state and church succeeded and failed in doing in Germany in the last two generations must, nevertheless, keep three things in mind: first, that only in the 1850's did Germany slowly begin to become an industrialized country, and only those persons who had become acquainted with the more complex conditions in England could have a presentiment of the implications of this fact; second, that just in those years in which the labor movement grew up, the more pressing problem of external politics pushed every other concern into the background for the leader of the government; and third, that the attitude of Social Democrats toward this state made the solution not a little more difficult, indeed made it impossible.[56] It was surely a great misfortune that the German Social Democrats did not produce or even encourage a single leader who, thinking beyond Marx, might have found practicable means to satisfy the legitimate demands of the workers. Here too, Marxist orthodoxy, the unfortunate counterpart of the Christian orthodoxy of the seventeenth century, stifled the German Social Democratic movement's sense of realism.

From the beginning Calvinism attacked the social problem with greater vigor. Calvin considered the deaconate one of the four offices that were essential for an orderly congregation, and thus from the beginning he impressed upon his church its unceasing obligation for its poor. The difficulties that he had to overcome in establishing the office of the deacon in Geneva were no less formidable than elsewhere. If one reads the very complex instructions for the deacons in the *Ordonnances ecclésiastiques* one realizes that circumstances in Geneva were the same as in every German city: appropriations of specified funds for the city hospital and their administration by city employees. Despite this, Calvin succeeded in making the deacons feel as representatives of the church, even though the city had a voice in their selection. As contrasted with Luther, he also found the people to fill this office; for he knew how to make activity in the church a matter of pride. In addition, the arrangement that he instituted for regular home visits, which brought the pastor into personal contact with each individual member of his congregation, always gave opportunity to check on the work of the deaconate and to set it into relationship with spiritual activity. Consequently wherever Calvinism spread, in France, Holland, Scotland, the Lower Rhine, there arose a well-organized ecclesiastical poor relief. It was distinguished not so much by its magnificent institutions, which it created especially in Holland, but even more by the spirit that dominated it. The best characteristics of Calvin, the rare combination of delicate refinement and educational determination, became evident in these activities of the Reformed Church.[57]

But even Calvinism kept itself consciously within a definite limit in its work. It considered poor relief, indeed charity as such, not only a duty but also a privilege of the church and omitted, therefore, until late in the nineteenth century, to influence the state and its social legislation. At the beginning of the nineteenth century the principles of this point of view were represented and thoroughly defined by the most important social leader that Calvinism produced, Thomas Chalmers. Chalmers passionately opposed the introduction of British poor law in Scotland. But in his reorganized relief program in Glasgow he demonstrated that a purely ecclesiastical welfare program was possible even under the more complex conditions of modern times and among a laboring population in restless ferment, and that it could meet all the existing needs. At the same time he sought to give a rigorous scientific proof that only ecclesiastical charity was really in a position to help the oppressed. He attacked the problem at the point that in the Reformers' evaluation of work appeared most important and at which, in fact, the most serious difficulty existed, the obligation to maintain or even to increase the sense of honor and personal will power among the recipients of charity.[58] He thought every nonecclesiastical charity would founder on this obligation. For mere relief, always, whether as alms or as a public dole, corrupts the recipient because it shames him and in the long run dulls his sense of self-respect. Christian charity has the opposite effect; it enhances self-respect because it is a personal service and creates a personal relationship that encourages the oppressed. In an enhanced self-respect Chalmers also saw, however, the decisive condition for the economic improvement of the working class. But he surrenders the economic struggle itself, the encounter with the employer, completely to the worker. He indeed allows the worker liberties unheard of at that time. It was astonishing that a man in his position defended not only the trade unions but also declared that there were no moral arguments against the strike. But Chalmers was convinced, and believed that he could also demonstrate it economically, that the advantages won in all these ways would not benefit the worker as long as he was not in a position to discipline himself morally and hereby inspire public respect. For the entrepreneur possesses the power to change every wage increase won by the worker into a hollow victory. But the entrepreneurial class could not forever resist the pressure that would come from a morally elevated labor movement.

Because of these views Karl Marx portrayed Chalmers as a narrow parson. But this much at least his example proved: that an ecclesiastical benevolence—practiced in the elevated sense of Chalmers—was indispensable in addition to all public regulation of conditions, indeed was more important. Whoever does not wish to share the faith of social democracy derived from the Enlightenment, that the improvement of external conditions in the socialistic state by itself would raise men spiritually to a higher state and at one stroke inspire them with mutual love, will see the Reformed conception not indeed as a total solution, but as an emphasis with an indispensable truth.

England went its own way completely. Here a serious effort was made to establish the precept, "There shall be no poor among you." This was the intention of the Poor Law, which Elizabeth (on the basis of an initial effort under Henry VIII) promulgated in 1601. The parish, which was both a religious and a civil community, was made responsible for the resident poor within its bounds. At the same time it received the right to levy a tax for this purpose. To hinder the abuse of relief by slackers the workhouse was soon added to complete the arrangements. Here the poor could be referred and here, in addition, orphans were to be reared. However helpful the intent, the actuality was horrifying. The workhouse became a place for the abuse of adults and children and an opportunity for the shameless exploitation of defenseless labor by greedy entrepreneurs. And the worst of it was that, as a result of this organization of charity, the social conscience of the English people as good as fell asleep. One believed to have done his

Christian duty when he paid the burdensome poor tax, which was forced up more by the hunger for profits of entrepreneurs than by the increase in poverty. The century that boasted of the civil and human rights that it had won did nothing for the human rights of these poor. Even the great religious reform movement of the eighteenth century, Methodism, passed heedlessly by this crying need.

Only at the turn of the eighteenth century, as the dark side of the powerful growth of industry and the horrible improverishment of the fourth estate were made glaringly clear, did a change occur. But not because of the representatives of the state church; for neither the little group of the Hakney Phalanx nor that part of the evangelicals who were warming up to social issues carried any weight. The sects did just as little; the Quakers were an exception among them. Among the broad masses of the members of the state church and especially among the members of the sects that conception of Christianity was much more effective which saw it as a completely personal, purely inner affair, an involuntary or, as among the Puritans and Methodists, even a deliberate withdrawal from these questions. The great campaigns for the reform of the Poor Law, for limiting the work of women and children, were led by liberal politicians and economists,

at their head men like Owen. Within the church
it required the bold work of Maurice, Irving,
Arnold, Robertson, and Kingsley to rouse the
social conscience. In the period that followed,
it was the high church wing especially that
threw itself vigorously into this work. But even
after it laid aside its diffidence, the Anglican
church did not go beyond certain definite and
revealing limits. Just as in Calvinism, England,
too, surrendered the defense of the economic
demands of the workers in the main to the
workers or to the political parties. The church
provided no leaders for this struggle. But it did
intervene at important moments, especially in
wage disputes, through its bishops as arbiters
to some degree, and the judgment that it there
pronounced customarily carried weight even in
public life as the verdict of an impartial
authority. It supplied its direct help, falling
back into Catholicism at this point, too, exclusively to the poor and the unfortunate. And
even this was not done officially, but in the
form of voluntary charity, carried out primarily by high church orders. Consequently,
despite wealthy means and despite much personal sacrifice in the face of actual need, the
results were inadequate.

Booth was the first among leaders of the
sects—after he had for a generation worked
exclusively with souls—effectively to break

through the dominant prejudice. He had the unique merit of discovering the fifth estate. Yet he, too, remained an Englishman in both the goals and the methods of his social work. He did not think of raising the fifth estate as such, but only of snatching as many individuals as possible from misery. And the means that he used were, in the last analysis, like Chalmers's, moral influence, the reawakening of a sense of self-respect. For the best that the Salvation Army achieves in a social sense is that it restores a sense of self-respect to the social outcast by taking him into its community and that it teaches him to value this treasure. But Booth thereby once again proved the help of the church indispensable. For in his work it is finally clear that actually only a church is in a position to bring about the spiritual rehabilitation of the unfortunate. In any event, Booth in his own way achieved for thousands what the workhouse never accomplished, the restoration of joy in work.

III. EFFECTS ON EDUCATION, HISTORY, PHILOSOPHY, POETRY, AND ART

When one moves from these basic matters to the realm of higher culture, it appears more difficult in the very complex contemporary spiritual life—which has been formed by widely differing impulses—to identify those elements derived from the Reformation. Nevertheless, the spiritual peculiarities of the Reformation are so sharply defined that its contribution is everywhere clearly etched.

That the Reformation concerned itself with higher culture at all and included cultural strivings among its goals from the beginning was already demanded by its religious point of origin. For it was indeed not an enthusiastic movement expecting its assurance of God through a direct bestowal of the spirit. Instead, by referring the individual to the Bible, a not inconsequential measure of knowledge, of examining something historically given, was included in the religious experience itself. And further, how should one be in a position to exercise the rights of the universal priesthood, i.e., to maintain his independent judgment in the highest ethical and religious questions, if he was not educated for this purpose? Not only was the education of the will necessary for this end, but also a universal education of the intellect. Everyone must at least be brought to the point where he could read the Bible and draw independent instruction from it. And as a support for this, the church had to possess systematic knowledge that could solve scholarly problems and give instruction in the disciplined use of the Bible.

From this basis the Reformation advances next to the demand for a universal public school. The progress that it fostered at this point is manifest and clear to see. It first of all set itself the goal, which no one, least of all the humanists, had considered before, namely, to reach everyone systematically through schools. Consequently, from 1523 on Luther promoted the establishment of schools.[1] Note-worthily, even for girls. And to accomplish something for them in his town of Wittenberg in 1527 he made room and board available in his house for a woman to teach in a school for girls.[2] But Luther further instructed the government explicitly that the state had no less a responsibility in the support of schools than the church. Indeed, as it is difficult to persuade the common man of the utility and necessity of such things, Luther had no scruples in taking a stand for compulsory public education.[3] As soon as there was a reorganization of church affairs, this matter was therefore also drawn into the plans. The Saxon church visitation of 1527 already places the organization of schools alongside the organization of churches. Thereafter, as the Reformation was introduced in the different territories, both occur together as characteristic of Protestantism.

Calvin made the tie of the church with the school an even closer one. He counted the doctor, i.e., the teacher, among the four officers of the church. Thus even more definite expression was given the position that the organization of the church cannot be counted as complete unless provisions are made at the same time for a school. In France, accordingly, not only the congregation, but also the nobility were obligated to provide instruction for the children of their people. There at the beginning of the seventeenth century one encounters, in the synods, resolutions that each province must have at least one secondary school. Even in otherwise backward Scotland, Calvinism insists on its demands.

This was not just a matter of paper resolves. If one applies modest standards, one can only wonder at how quickly the Reformation approached its goal. By the end of the sixteenth century in Germany a number of territories, Saxony, Hesse, Württemberg, had a flourishing public school system. After the Thirty Years' War under the influence of the expanding Pietism a new growth of schools followed.

The education imparted in these schools had a strong religious accent; it was, if you please, narrow in so far as it aimed at recruiting for orthodoxy. But it does not deserve the contempt with which later generations believed they could look down upon it. What orthodoxy gave youth with its emphasis on memorization, meditation, and comparison of Bible passages was a mental discipline of the first order. And it bore fruit. Without this education the great and universal progress that Germany made during the Enlightenment would have been quite unthinkable. In France the effects of the school education demanded by the Reformation are perhaps even more directly apparent. For the assurance with which even the ordinary Huguenot carried on intellectual controversy with scholarly opponents may properly call forth a certain amount of astonishment. The pre-eminence of the religious, moreover, brought a further advantage, namely, that every advance made in this discipline worked out its effect in new principles for education. When Pietism deepened religion into the personal and emphasized individual experience, it wasted no time in directing public school ordinances toward this goal. Nor was A. H. Francke the first, but rather the beginnings were made by Ernest the Pious of Gotha.

In the same way the Reformation, if it wished to develop a pre-eminent body of knowledge, had to work within the schools for the development of levels of instruction. With this in mind Luther insists that the urban schools, which in this way excel the territorial, give instruction in Latin.[4] Even in the worship service he would gladly have kept certain Latin portions for the sake of such scholars.[5] He gave good reasons to justify this additional demand, which to the ordinary citizen may have seemed superfluous. The most revealing reason was that only by the study of a foreign language did understanding of one's native tongue really develop. But this division into grades does not quite satisfy him. In addition to the common school he proposes special instruction for the "exceptional student"; one would today call it a school for superior students.[6] This last idea also found its realization as well as the others. The organization of education instituted by the visitors incorporated this proposal,[7] and out of it also grew up the Saxon electoral schools and the Württemberg seminaries and foundation. Calvinism drew even finer distinctions. There, in connection with the founding of the Geneva Academy, the line of demarcation between secondary school and university was sharply drawn for the first time, and at the same time, development of classes according to plan was carried out within the secondary school.

The emphasis on language indicates the connection with the educational goals of humanism. Its insistence on "eloquence," on the clarity of thought and on the art of oratory must have seemed to Protestantism something to which it had affinity. In addition, too, the cultivation of grammar could only be welcomed by Protestantism, since it considered the "grammatical" interpretation of the Bible, in contrast to the fourfold meaning, the only valid method.

But within what they had in common certain traits do stand out sharply, which distinguish the educational goals of Protestantism from those of humanism. Something more than a multiplication of subject matter was involved when Protestantism, for the sake of the Bible, demanded the study of Hebrew with the same emphasis as the two classical languages. Flacius wrote a separate monograph to arouse in the theologians a particular sense of obligation for learning Hebrew. The growth in the knowledge of Oriental languages since the sixteenth century manifestly goes back in the first instance to Protestantism, just as it was also carried chiefly by it in the following period. That a man was "a master of three languages," a rare achievement in the age of humanism, became something quite commonplace in Protestantism in the course of a few generations. The conquest of this new area, nevertheless, benefited general philology and the knowledge of languages as such. When the evangelical theologian put the Old and New Testaments side by side to explain them in their original language, he encountered at all points the difference between the structure and spirit of the classical and Oriental languages. Soon he discovered that figurative speech, the art of rhetoric and the forms of poetry, even sentence structure and connection, were different in the two languages. Flacius had already reached highly important observations in his *Clavis*. The evangelical theologian constantly felt himself required for the sake of the Bible again and again to continue this research and to develop sensitivity for the uniqueness of linguistic expression.

Nor did Protestants join the one-sided emphasis on form. Luther took some pleasure in calling himself a barbarian before the true humanists, although he actually wrote a fluent Latin. But he nevertheless evaluated the classical authors from a perspective different from that of the average humanist. When later in life he deplored that in his youth he had not read more poets and historians, he was not thinking of the refinement of his Latin style, which he could have achieved in other ways, but of the enrichment of the knowledge of life, which he had thus lost. "Much time is required for personal experience." One shortens his course and avoids many errors when he learns from authors, and that means from history. For this reason, despite objectionable matter contained in them, he did not wish to omit even the comic poets, Terence and Plautus, in school because in them real life and real people are so excellently portrayed. Melanchthon himself inclined more strongly toward "Ciceronianism," so strongly that at times the Strasbourgers found it too much. But again it was the Bible that forced him to turn from form to content. Whoever wishes to interpret the Bible must know something of everything that is mentioned in it, plants, minerals, and animals, geography and ancient history. Luther had already discovered this while translating the Bible, and consequently, in contrast to the scholastics, emphasized the necessity of such studies.[8] Melanchthon elevated this insight to an academic rule in that in working out the Wittenberg Statutes he specifically gave the pre-theological studies in the arts faculty an

orientation toward this goal. Impulses thus
arose that led many a man deeper into these related areas. Orthodox theologians, about whom
one would not otherwise believe it, such as Mey-
fart and Calov, espoused geography with affec-
tion and success. It was, therefore, no simple in-
novation, but only a stronger emphasis on what
had already been practiced when Pietism later
in alliance with John Amos Comenius laid emphasis on practical knowledge in education.

Of the specific intellectual disciplines, apart
from theology, history[9] stood closest to the
Reformation. In this area a new and important
obligation manifested itself directly. The
Reformation did not just quibble like the
Renaissance over a few points of tradition or
direct consideration only to a particular area
like political history. For it the whole historical
picture that formerly had been definitive for
Christendom, and which was most closely
allied with the self-awareness of the European
nations, just collapsed. But it also felt the imperative need for rebuilding the ruins. For only
as it developed a picture of history which cor-
responded to its point of view could it justify
itself, and even more importantly, God's action
in history. By working on this tremendous task
Protestantism sharpened its understanding for
history. The knowledge it gained, in turn, enriched greatly the general science of history.

Yet, it certainly meant no restriction on research if Protestantism retained that "transcendental" point of view today so roundly condemned by secular historians and the Marxists. For most important for it was the meaning, the divine meaning of history. The consideration of the transcendental in this instance, however, only sharpened the eye for the factual. In order to discover in history the meaning that it saw before its eyes, the Reformation had to immerse itself in the materials and work them through anew from beginning to end. In the gigantic work of the Magdeburg Centuriators the Reformation made its first effort. It is no small testimony for the intellectual powers of its originators and for the strength of the impulses that lay in the Reformation that, as early as this first effort, matters of significance for the general progress of historical science were brought into the light of day.

What was new in this was the determination of the subject matter of history. Flacius expressed himself on this in the preface to the Magdeburg "Centuries." He reproaches his predecessors that they were all of them only personal historians, writers, he would say, who conceived of history only as a succession of individual personalities and a mass of anecdotes. He, on the contrary, wished to follow through the major motifs that portray the history of doctrine, of polity, of piety, and so forth, in their whole development. It is the recognition of the significance of the substance of history, the insight that what is actually significant are the forms that a particular community or a particular age evolves, which breaks through here. At the same time it became apparent that it was not only his own personal genius that led Flacius to this new point of view. It arose with a certain inner necessity out of the situation in which the Reformation found itself over against the Catholic Church. If it wished to bring forth the evidence for its historical justification, it could not do so effectively through individual instances of truth—Flacius originally started in this way[10]—but only from the historical circumstances themselves. It had to compare itself as a whole with the totality of the Catholic Church, to clarify for itself the forms of life flowing from the essence of the church and to follow their development through the centuries. To be the first to understand this is the great service of Flacius, and in so far as contemporary historiography seeks similar goals, it stands on his shoulders, consciously or unconsciously.

No less incisive was the position the Reformation took toward the sources of history. What the Renaissance did only in individual

instances, which accidentally came to the attention of the research workers, the Reformation
did as a matter of principle. Every original
source, every fact to which the Catholic Church
appealed, the Reformation felt obligated to
examine. The scientific procedure according to
which this was to be done, on the basis of
inspired beginnings by Luther, Calvin, and the
authors of "the Centuries," was developed
further, particularly in the French church of
the seventeenth century. But not only through
the Maurists, whom the textbook historians
alone know, and who serve learned half-knowl-
edge as a sort of collective term for everything that was happening in France at the
time. As if there did not exist, alongside of
and even before the great Maurists, on the
Protestant side a Du Plessis-Mournay, a Blon-
del, a Vasa, and especially the unique Daillé,
the author of so many and such effective works.
Whoever has learned the intellectual history of
seventeenth-century France not only from the
manuals, but also senses something of the connection of scientific work with the ecclesiastical
questions that were prominent at the time, will
also know that only the aggravation of opposition, the necessity of discussion with equal—
or victorious—Reformed adversaries, coerced
the Catholic side also into a strictness of procedure, which, taking its beginning from

theology, became a part of a common intellectual possession. In addition, what was accomplished at this stage was always first of all the art of deciding between genuine and spurious sources.

The further development of the treatment of source materials belongs exclusively to Protestantism, and it was once again a religious-ecclesiastical question that occasioned it. As a result of the experience that Pietism itself had with the official condemnation of highly sincere persons as heretics, Gottfried Arnold became suspicious of official presentations of history in general. He therefore demanded that all church history investigate everywhere the intent of a report—including, indeed especially, a contemporary one—that it discuss to what extent party position and personal consideration played a role in its composition. This was the thought which, with its exaggerated bias removed, led to the source criticism of an F. O. Baur and a Ranke. But it is also apparent at this point how, beside the external situation of Pietism, the reawakened awareness of the universal priesthood, as against the officeholder, and Pietism's deepened understanding for living persons, played an outstanding part in this discovery.

Nevertheless, the evaluation of the source remains only a preliminary to the conception of history itself. More important than the evaluation is the understanding of the source. Here again Luther gave the decisive impulse. For he is the actual inventor of the method of arriving at sympathetic understanding. But he did not see this method—whose achievement on his part rested as much on a fortunate natural disposition as on long and earnest practice—as an advantage with which he could excel others: he viewed it as something that every Christian must learn for the sake of the Bible and from the Bible. According to him, the Word of God was only understood when the reader of the text was inwardly affected by it and received a corresponding attitude to it, so that the content of the Word became alive in the believer himself. It was necessary to push from the word to the content, and from the content to understand the word. This demand includes a definite presupposition, whose clear explication brought about further important progress. Over against the Catholic Church and the enthusiasts, who both asserted the "obscurity" of the Holy Scriptures, Luther stood for the fundamental principle of the self-interpreting clarity of the Bible and give it an impressive emphasis in the formula: *Scriptura sacra sui ipsius interpres.* What he determined by this formula went far beyond theology in its effect; it reached out to include all historical interpretation. For never had it been expressed so bluntly and openly that a source must in every case be explained from its own content. When Luther added this second kind of understanding from within to the grammatical understanding, the two united in the recognition that all genuine interpretation, yes, even all translation, is a reworking, a reproduction of what is given in the text.

The Lutheran Church has preserved this heritage faithfully. Since Flacius's *Clavis* the pedagogical art of interpretation has remained a much cultivated discipline in Protestantism, and the analysis always points to the problem of reaching this inner understanding of the text. The Calvinist Church did not lag behind the Lutheran in this; there the commentaries of Calvin already supplied a point of departure for a brilliant development of the art of interpretation.

In the effort to understand the text from within—which at the same time also gave interpretation a direction toward unity and toward completeness—theological exegesis had an advantage which, despite all dogmatic entanglement, elevated it far beyond contemporary philological interpretation. For here even in great interpreters like Scaliger the treatment of the text lost itself in details, details for the most part of an archaeological nature. The full

development of the seed planted by Luther in
theology was first reached at the moment when
a great body of literature arose in Germany,
and out of the impulse of creation it grew into
perfection in the course of the development
from Klopstock to the romantics. But, as its
origins still show, even this stage of the development is tied to Luther. For it was in
studying the Bible, even in the same places
where Luther had first discovered the beauty
of the Old Testament, that the reinvigorators
of this art, Klopstock, Hamann, and Herder,
awakened their perception for it. Thus a steady
line moves from Luther to neo-humanism and
on to the romantics.

Meanwhile, indeed, the manner in which
historians perceived the subject matter of history and the task of historical research had
changed thoroughly. The Reformation had
looked upon the church as the goal of history
and that which gave the totality of historical
materials their integral form. By church it
understood the invisible church, the kingdom of
God. But it could not, indeed, avoid setting the
visible church, i.e., its own church, in a particularly close relationship to that invisible subject. After the Thirty Years' War the Enlightenment removed the church, Evangelical as well
as Catholic, from this dominant position.
Originally it replaced it with the state. But the

further, more far-reaching point of view developed out of the Enlightenment, which then dissolved the state once again in society. In Comte and Karl Marx this development appears to be completed. A change in research methods went hand in hand with this change in the subject of history. While the development did not lead in this direction necessarily, in actuality it was overwhelmingly true that those who in their research emphasized the "scientific" character more and more pushed aside the "transcendental," i.e., finally not only the idea of God, but also the idea of purpose. The duty of historians to reproduce only the raw facts seemed to demand that science limit itself to the determination of the chain of causation, according to the slogan popular today, to illuminate "sociologically" the historical conditions according to which in each case the higher forms of society and state in their present determination proceed from the simple communal forms of primitive times.

As a matter of fact, even this research, which claimed to deny itself all value judgments, could not avoid secretly or consciously taking a value judgment or a dream of the future as a guiding motif of its work. It requires this even in the analysis of facts and finally, then, when it is necessary to arrange the individual social forces, in some sort of "order." From this situation it follows, however, that the value judgments inherited from the past, sometimes from the religious past, unconsciously continued their influence into an era that thought itself to have gone completely beyond them. The Enlightenment set as its desired goal, by which it judged history, the idea of a perfected human race. It believed to be able to derive this directly from reason. But just as in itself even the idea of a pure humanity and a pure human community is only a translation of the Christian into the secular, so indeed the hidden influence of their religious convictions is most apparent in its specific development within the individual nations.

For the German interpretation it was noteworthy that Leibniz liked to describe the goal of history with the term taken from Luther, the kingdom of God. In doing so, to be sure, he thoroughly emptied Luther's concept of the kingdom of its meaning. But it was nevertheless important that he introduced this concept, with which contemporary theologians no longer knew how to deal, into the philosophy of German idealism and raised it to the place of a major concept; even more, that thereby he supported the interpretation of the idea of mankind in personal moral terms and as a spiritual community. Unmistakably Leibniz thereby held fast to the line of development coming out of the Reformation. Kant deepened this point of view even more and at the same time tied himself more closely to the Lutheran tradition. For his conception of human dignity as resting on submission to an unconditioned law leads in its rigor even more definitely back to Luther. It signifies for the conception of history the rejection of the concepts of happiness and welfare, which the Enlightenment treated as the highest measures of value, and the emphasis on the inner, on that which is won through self-control, as truly cultural over against a mere refinement of culture or a mere reconstruction of outer circumstances.

Thereby the German view differentiated itself not only from the French, in which emphasis fell particularly on the latter, but also from that dominant in England. There, indeed, in contrast to Hobbes—who was able to see the establishment of social order only as the victory of reason, which saw its advantage more clearly, over natural impulse—Locke and Shaftesbury occupied themselves with the ennobling of the idea of humanity and the concept of the human community. From a dominant egotism they derive feelings of benevolence, and Shaftesbury sought to establish these feelings in their own right by reference to aesthetic standards (harmony). But the social order, which on the above grounds one regarded as a desired goal, included (besides freedom in the form of political human rights) only an assurance of "happiness" for each individual in the particular English meaning of the word, i.e., promoting the possibility for successful business activity.

Thereafter the difference is measured in the conception of the course of history. Luther's heritage maintained itself in Germany through the conviction that history has a moral goal; the faith in something unconditioned, which must be willed even at the price of happiness, and which is accomplished in history; the assumption that the moral forces are ultimately decisive; and, most profoundly, the insight that history is, in truth, not the work of man, but of the power directing him. This is the manner in which Hegel, Ranke, and Treitschke interpreted history. Related to this view of history is that of Carlyle, who himself—despite his break with dogma—was well aware of his connection with the faith of his church. One feels that uniquely Calvinistic emphasis, when, more sharply than the Germans, he singles out the significance of the great man, the divinely called hero, who, as the instrument of God and herald of a new order, has the inner right to achieve his will even with severity, because such severity is true love to those who require his leadership.

With this explanation we have transgressed on the question of the relationship of the Reformation to the modern philosophy that follows it. A certain basic tension has always existed between these two forces, in spite of the fact that the Reformation was an important factor in re-establishing the independence of philosophy. For it not only broke up the unified church-dominated world view prevailing until then, thereby encouraging a method of reflection free from dogma; but even the very basis of the new philosophy, namely, its autonomy, found support in the Reformation's emphasis on personal conscience and the value of personal experience. But the new philosophy did not arise from religious sources. The impetus for it came rather from the newly discovered scientific facts and its appearance actually signified the dethronement of theology. The exclusive privilege that theology claimed up to that time to formulate world views is now challenged by a reason that feels it has come of age, which through its immersion in reality wishes to force its way independently to the secret of the cosmos. But the same observation that has just been made about history remains true here, even in greater measure. Even less than a closed historical viewpoint does a world view spring forth from pure reason or from the mere analysis of the facts. A world view always includes a personal position, a judgment of the totality of things which is never a simple consequence of a survey of the facts, but always, at the same time, is conditioned by the desires and inner necessities of the research worker, by the direction and the power of his volition. What the philosopher, in distinction to the pure scientist, regards as "reality" is always a selection, a right ordering of the actually given, an evaluation, behind which, ultimately, a determinate will is hidden. And this will itself is in every instance formed partly by tradition, especially the religious tradition, even when it thinks itself completely free.

Unfortunately there exists for this discipline as yet no history of philosophy which traces the influence of Luther on German idealism with the same care that has been used in tracing the influence of scholasticism on Hobbes, Spinoza, and Leibniz. What can be offered here is obviously no more than a crude outline that draws attention to a few major lines of influence.

The clear dependence on the Lutheran tradition of Leibniz, the founder of German idealism, is most apparent, even in the purely philosophical development of thought. For him there were good factual reasons to portray the relatedness of the world as something produced by thought, not by mechanical action. For only thought can join the separated, while the purely material breaks into pieces. Leibniz thereby not only secured the idea of God philosophically, but with reference to the spiritual significance of phenomena he gave the impetus to a movement that can be followed through the whole subsequent development of German idealism. But that being must therefore also be present exclusively in the form of spiritual unities, locked in themselves—an assumption that forced Leibniz to the dubious discovery of pre-established harmony—was not to be deduced from this fundamental idea. This faith, for it is no more, was possible for Leibniz only because of the deeply impressed conviction, deriving from Luther, of the unique, the sole worth of personal existence.

The relationship to Luther is even more clearly revealed in connection with the personal attitude toward the world and its events. The philosophical reasons that Leibniz offers for his opinions actually are nowhere sufficient. He could neither demonstrate that this is the best of all possible worlds, nor could he show on the basis of the arguments of pure reason why man, if this world is only relatively the best, should accept everything in it, even evil, with inner assent. Nevertheless, Leibniz explicitly made the latter demand in conscious opposition to

Descartes and to a stoic dumb resignation, one may add, even in distinction from a resigned renunciation that in Spinoza is the obverse of his *amor dei intellectualis*. What Leibniz demands on his part, a voluntary acceptance of destiny, is, indeed, no other than the attitude that Luther in his debate with Catholic moral theory held up as the true meaning of Christian patience. The church in which he grew up and which, moreover, placed an especially strong emphasis on this aspect of its piety during the sufferings of the Thirty Years' War, taught Leibniz that the idea of God, as soon as it is taken seriously, includes the obligation to assent joyfully to whatever God sends. Leibniz thereby proved that he had more understanding of true religion than other representatives of the Enlightenment, who, like Voltaire, defended the word of "God" without thinking of the serious practical consequences—but it was his religion alone, not his philosophy, that provided Leibniz with this attitude. Nevertheless, it was just this philosophically undemonstrable assumption (this is itself evidence for our contention)—that a true philosophy must lead to a clear affirmation of the world—that became an axiom that all of German idealism (Schopenhauer excepted) appropriated.

In other respects Leibniz stands in opposition to Luther. He was able to assert his optimism philosophically only in such a manner that he diluted or explained away any contradictory aspects of empirical reality. He deals with wickedness only as a special case of evil and attempts to understand evil itself as the necessary obverse of determinate individuality and therefore as a condition of the perfection of the world. But of what Leibniz suppressed, Jacob Böhme made a decisive issue. It is unnecessary to offer explicit proof that Luther provided the stimulus for Böhme. His idea of God, which places the contradiction, the "suffering" in God himself, is in fact nothing else than the speculative development of the Lutheran juxtaposition of wrath and love in God. Luther himself would, indeed, have strongly resisted the temptation to transform the opposition of wrath and love—in his thinking this referred to a single autonomous purposive will—into something metaphysical, and thus to subject God himself to a natural necessity. But the fact remains that Böhme won recognition for uniquely Lutheran impulses in German idealistic philosophy. Where Leibniz saw only smooth transition, Böhme agrees with Luther in the determination of struggle and contradiction. Over against an aesthetic viewpoint (Giordano Bruno) that allied itself with an overweening natural science, he, therefore, fully in the spirit of Luther, stood for the exclusive right of the world view that prefers a moral point of view. It is therefore no accident that in Lutheran circles, in so far as Lutheranism had a feeling for the speculative, Jacob Böhme always found followers, down to J. C. K. Hoffman and Martensen. For the historical consequences, it was indeed more important that, among the Württemberg Pietists, Ötinger espoused Böhme and developed his ideas further. From here Schelling received stimulation and on his part introduced Böhme into the great stream of German idealism.

Thus a startling light falls upon the great turning point in German philosophy at the end of the eighteenth century, the turn to a new metaphysics. It appears as the intersection of two lines, both of which go back to Luther. On the one side, there are Kant and Fichte who, in the spirit of Luther, deepened the Leibnizian idea of personality, and along with the concept of an unconditioned law, recovered the concept of sin. On the other side, there is Schelling, who had the gift to unite the speculative ideas derived from Böhme with this latter proposition. Thus there arises the great metaphysical question, with which German idealism concerned itself during its creative period, the obligation simultaneously to understand the absolute as transcending the contradiction that rules the world and yet to see it as that which again gives birth to contradiction. The Leibnizian-Lutheran belief that man's approach to the ultimate meaning of existence must be unconditionally positive is retained. At the same time, the irrational, particularly in the form of evil, is experienced more strongly. The ensuing result is the application to philosophy of the Lutheran formula of God's revelation in His very differentness and even in His contradiction. It was not without reason that Hegel liked to refer to the Lutheran dogma.

But Luther's influence reaches even into that philosophy which, in contrast to the prevailing mood, rejects a rational world view. Schopenhauer did more than all of German idealism to clear the air of the naïve belief of the Enlightenment which holds that the world is designed for man's happiness. Still, he did indirectly accept its postulates by saying that if the world had a meaning it would necessarily have to be designed for happiness. It is for this reason that Schopenhauer finds the world disappointing. Pain outweighs pleasure by far. But by inquiring into man's real and present striving for pleasure, he pays, in his own way, full homage to Luther. He sees the will as the ultimate in man and he describes this will just as it is found in reality, uninfluenced by metaphysical speculations or the kind-hearted concepts of the Enlightenment regarding man's goodness. But what he then determined about the will approaches surprisingly close to the Lutheran doctrine of original sin. For the discoveries to which he came: that there is an unconscious will, that the unconscious will is stronger than the conscious, that the will never wills anything other than itself—these are the characteristics of the "natural" will to which Luther had drawn attention in his doctrine of original sin. That Schopenhauer is here dependent on Luther is also verified by the judgment that he passes on this will. In and for itself his position did not make it at all necessary to call this blind will, which after all was natural, evil and to seek liberation from it, as Schopenhauer did in his own way. If he nevertheless took this path, then he, who felt himself the enemy of Christianity, has surrendered involuntarily to the power of an ecclesiastical, a Lutheran tradition.

Nietzsche turned away from Schopenhauer and in contrast to him requested an outright acclamation of the world and of life. Therewith, he returned into the fold of German idealism, without, however, finding it necessary to develop a suitable metaphysical basis. For him the existence of the will suffices as basis. The will is not will toward pleasure, but in clear rejection of Schopenhauer, will to power. Not to recognize it as such, or to suppress it, constitutes half-heartedness. But while Nietzsche thus condoned the natural instinct, he does not condone its cruelty. From the very beginning he searched for something that would serve to uplift the will to the level of an ideal. That he did this, that he strove toward a functional, useable morality was an accomplishment. What he preached was a resurgence of protest against the preceding age of materialism, its whining morality and its custom-bound routine; it was, it has to be said, a sort of return to German idealism. Nietzsche indeed sets his own morality, his "new tables of the law," in the sharpest opposition to Christianity and thus also to Luther; for this, Lutheranism, as it had developed, is not blameless. But the tables were not quite that new. The "superman," in which all of Nietzsche's philosophy is summarized, has his archetype not in the "genius" of the romantics or the men of power of the Renaissance, but in the "strong man" of the Apostle Paul and of Luther.[11] As certainly as Nietzsche hardly knew Luther's writings, one may nevertheless ask whether he could even have formulated his great concept of "Beyond Good and Evil," if in his youth he had never heard anything of the Pauline-Lutheran doctrine of "freedom from the law." In any case the traits with which he seeks to ennoble his superman—the contempt for fortune, courage for ethical daring, the consciousness of responsibility (how Nietzsche loved this word), the uniting of freedom and necessity in the highest acts, goodness, generous virtue, the willing acceptance and easy endurance of burdens, dancing in chains, hardness as love, that the divine is hidden under a mask—all these Nietzsche could not read from Cesare Borgia and Napoleon. He took it rather from the Christian tradition, which was still working in him; more clearly expressed, from the Lutheran conscience that was still active even in him. To appreciate this, one merely needs to compare him with the romantics. It was his particular and deeply tragic fate to have understood the heroic aspect of Luther's ethics far better than his contemporaries, yet to have felt compelled to take on the role of the Antichrist.[12]

Poetry frequently went hand in hand with philosophy in Protestantism, and particularly so in Germany. It is both the advantage and the limitation of German classical literature that it served not only for entertainment but also wanted to establish a world view.

Above all else, Luther gave poetry its language.[13] His German, the German of Luther's Bible, was the fountain at which the German language constantly refreshed itself when it was in danger of losing itself through the influence of a foreign language, Latin or French, or in an artificial literary style. And the biblical German worked even more directly on poetry because, along with his translation, Luther gave the generation that fed itself on this an abundance of pictures and perspectives. One need only remind oneself how often Bismarck, even in politics, used a word or a story from the Bible in order to clarify a situation or strike a particular mood at a single stroke. Only in Luther's translation could this impress itself so deeply.

Except for the chorale, the first one of the literary forms through which the Reformation gave something unique and gained influence on major literature is pre-eminently the letter. If one compares Luther's and Calvin's letters with those of contemporary humanists one gets an overwhelming impression of what a different spirit moved in the self-expression of the Reformers. Here we do not hear the voices of those who know how to flaunt their art in ornamental forms of speech and in select phrases, but we hear human beings who are concerned about issues and who therefore unconsciously give themselves. The religious movement, which they lived through, made them true and natural men again. Luther in particular is not ashamed to show himself in his full humanity whenever he feels he can thus deepen his personal relationship to his correspondent. The impetus that the Reformation thus gave, did not reach its full effect immediately. The advantage that humanism possessed in literary matters also because of its Latin education, showed itself strongly again in the next generation.

Pietism, however, seized the torn threads again. Within the history of literature it is as yet not sufficiently appreciated how great an impact this trend had on the development of German literature. Pietism created the first German literature of edification. Therewith, it paved the way for the German classic literature.

Other than Luther's, no literature of edification existed in Protestant Germany. As in all Protestant countries, its development was impeded by the exclusive reliance on the Bible as a means of edification. A true literature of edification developed only out of the movement that preceded Pietism, namely, Puritanism[14] in England and the ascetic trend it inspired in the Netherlands. It was from there that German Pietism—which certainly started before Spener —received the motivation to create its own characteristic writings.

The new piety that began with Pietism is characterized by a desire for articulation. It feels the urge to testify before others of its spiritual experience. And since this testimony addresses itself to everybody, it does so in German. Moreover, it does it in good German, formed by Luther's Bible, in refreshing contrast to the language of the scholars. For this reason alone, men like Grossgebauer and Luetkemann deserve a place in the history of literature.

Regarding content, this growing literature concerns itself with two points of view. For one thing, the belief in providence, which withstood the hard test of the Thirty Years' War, now stressed a devout concern with God's rule of the realm of external nature. One must not underestimate books like *Gottholds zufällige Andachten* (*Gottholds Incidental Devotions*), limited as they may seem to us today. In such books the trend that differentiates this piety from the more naïve one of the age of Reformation can be detected. The belief in providence of that time demands to see itself confirmed time and again and in every detail. For that reason it is also in principal agreement with the rising natural sciences; all the more so since men like Kepler were closing the gap from the other side. For all casual relationships and laws of nature that science may discover only enhance the glory of the Creator who so wisely ordered everything. Thus, almost imperceptibly, a new religious feeling for nature crystallizes, full of awe and admiration for the

eternal and yet unafraid to grasp the eternal
even in its minutest manifestations.

But the new piety has its greatest impact
when it speaks about itself and its own spiritual
experiences. Here Pietism aided in the development of specific types of literature. It established the letter as a regular religious art form
and thereby filled it with personal vitality in
the strongest contrast to the contemporary
French development, in which letter-writing under the influence of classicism was robbed of
everything directly personal, even of all content.
And not only the letter. The diary and the
autobiography stand alongside letter-writing in
Pietism. Pietism cultivated all these forms, for
they were indispensable as means for deepening
personal life. The individual clarifies and en-
riches his life by revealing himself to himself
and to others.

The Pietistic autobiography, which is the
climax of this minor literature, represents a
new stage in religious self-portrayal. From the
very beginning it is distinguished from all that
precedes by a trait that clearly betrays its
Lutheran origin. Through his conversion the
Pietist is indeed inwardly separated from the
world, but he nevertheless remains in the world
and in his customary calling. And though the
conversion takes place in a sudden act, it nevertheless appeared to be prepared for through a

development in his life in which external fate and inner movement are closely entwined. The interrelationship of the external and the internal, the emphasis on the external, on environment and the special situation, as a means by which God works, is the new and characteristic mark. This clearly reveals the Lutheran character of the Pietistic belief in providence. The author is thus obligated, as he follows the divine plan that moves through his life, to observe even minute details of the daily routine. In all of this the gentle knocking of grace is already to be discerned, a knocking that the person now converted—this is the dominant disposition—has often failed to hear. But the duty of gratitude to God demands that afterward even this originally weak effect must be brought into the foreground in order to shed light on divine patience and the wrestling of God for the human soul. Furthermore, Pietistic self-portrayal does not conclude with conversion. For with it the most important obligation of the new believer starts, to live henceforth completely according to God's purposes. This demands a sharpened attention to one's self. The diary, recording progress and regression, missed opportunities and the assistance of grace, offers the necessary support. Self-observation does not, however, remain lost in individual events. At great crises or at the end of life one might, indeed, like Petersen, trust himself to portray what God with his special leading had made of him.

Within the life of an individual certain particularly significant moments stand out as occasions in which it is necessary to reach a consequential decision. The question was whether it was possible to win "freedom," as the manner of speech had it, for a particular matter. Certainty could appear to the indecisive person either through an external sign or through a sudden overwhelming inner feeling which made a particular decision seem to be the one that God clearly desired. The impression which the actor had in both instances is that a higher transcendent being gives him instruction; but he nevertheless still faces the requirement to determine for himself afterward whether the decision reached was also actually the right one.

Finally the Pietist, because of the situation in which he finds himself over against the world, also possesses a keen eye for the life and business of his surroundings. For he faces the relentless obligation to spurn the temptations that press upon him from society and to oppose them with his particular style of life. It is therefore necessary also to observe this alien world sharply. And Pietism attained a certain mastery in its portrayal of its adversary.

One would seek in vain outside Pietistic literature for such lively portrayal of one's surroundings as, for example, Eleonore Petersen's.[15]

As soon as one becomes aware of these traits, one becomes aware of the forward movement that this modest literature contained and what impetus could flow from it.

This was important even for the choice of subject. In these biographies it became evident that not only those who stood on the heights had significant experiences. One did not need to be a king or a general to be a "hero." Even from ordinary bourgeois life one could fetch something important, something that moved the feelings, if one only had eyes to see and the depth of sensitivity to bring it to the surface.

From these examples one learned first of all truly to observe human beings. The conceptual analysis of man in Hobbes and Spinoza appears stiff beside these self-portraits. The universal concept of man is now dissolved. The recognition gains ground that each person is a separate being who has his own world and experiences events in it as no one else can experience them.

And what riches revealed themselves in the inner life of the individual! One now obtained a picture of the growth of character, of the crises through which a development moves, of the collaboration of external events and inner unfolding. But what was most important was that through this one became attentive to the significance of the subconscious and the unconscious in the inner life of man. Leibniz had already sensed something of this, but he knew the distinction of consciousness only as a distinction in "representation." Pietism saw deeper: it saw the gradations of volition and knew something of the fact that what lies behind consciousness, the dark urges, may be more important for the formation of the real will than the reasons with which the individual justifies his actions to himself and others.

From these stimuli the new novel arose. From this origin it retained in Germany the peculiarity that the emphasis always fell on spiritual development. The profit that lyric poetry drew from the progress here described one can learn from Christian Günther, the first German writer after Flemming who knew how to express inner feeling in a way true to life. For drama there arose, finally, not only the possibility of deepening its characters and explaining the denouement as arising from the interrelationship of conscious reflection and hidden impulse, but also a new conception of poetic justice. The hero meets his fate not merely by chance, not only through external causes. What happens to him can happen only to him and *must* happen to him; his fate is not accidental; he has brought it on himself.

It is customarily held to be the dark side of the Reformation that it did not devote the requisite attention of art—with the exception of music, where its creativity is undeniable—indeed, that it even discouraged art. One has heard something of the destruction of sculpture—in the judgment of which modern aesthetes regularly forget that for the Catholic Church the images were not, as for them, mere works of art, mere symbols, but representations of reality and objects of veneration—and one understands profoundly how to prove from the essence of Protestantism that it was a religion purely devoted to the spiritual, the intellectual, and thus that it was hostile to everything sensuous.

In principle a single look at Luther ought to suffice to disprove such superficialities. In every line that Luther wrote it is apparent what unusual compulsion toward imagery possessed him and what joy it gave him to picture events before his own eyes and those of others. If one compares the scholastics with him, it may with much more right be said that only with Luther did religious perception come into its own as inner perception. And was there not inspiration enough to move an artist in the form in which

Luther in his translation brought the biblical stories, which he first made generally available, closer to the inner experience of his readers? Even among the Calvinists, hostile to art as they were, it was precisely the Huguenots who further developed the old mystery plays as edifying dramas in the direction of the new dramatic art.[16] A desire to see things before them must also have been present among them.

If Protestantism lagged for such a long time in the one art whose work is most visible, in architecture, there were special reasons. First of all, the existing churches that Protestantism took over sufficed for its needs. For centuries there was no occasion to build new ones. But at this point there was also an inner obstacle. The fact that in the worship service Luther had not really created anything new, but had been content with a purification of tradition, long prevented Protestantism from reaching clarity over the purpose of the church building. What ends should it really serve? It could not be a house of God in the Catholic sense. For there was here no sacrament to be revered. Should it then be a preaching place or a place for meditation? Or both together? So long as these questions were not decided, indeed, not even discussed, Protestantism was not in a position to give artists assured direction. But as soon as a period came that felt itself clear on this subject—it was the sober period of the eighteenth century—Protestantism brought forth its own style of church architecture. One may judge this style as he wishes; it was a style.

In the domain of painting and sculpture the Reformation from the beginning announced a definite taste that represented a transformation of what had preceded. Luther himself expressed this opinion unambiguously. Frequently and gladly he referred in his discussion of images to "how the painters paint"; so often that it would pay someone to collect his remarks. Rarely, however, did he not indicate a certain dissatisfaction. What he missed in the customary representations and how he wished religious subjects treated, he expressed most clearly in the passage on the Magnificat. He censures "the masters who so depict and portray the blessed Virgin that there is found in her nothing to be despised, but only great and lofty things"; instead, in his opinion, they should portray "how the exceeding riches of God joined in her with her utter poverty, the divine honor with her low estate, the divine glory with her shame, the divine greatness with her smallness, the divine goodness with her lack of merit, the divine grace with her unworthiness." No lengthy exposition is necessary to show that these desires are consistent with Luther's most profound religious views. For him it appears to be both the duty of art and therefore also its beauty to show in religious art how the divine, the sublime, appears precisely in the improbable, in the contemptible. For in human weakness and nothingness God's power is particularly revealed. This was explicit opposition to the "tinsel and noise," the attention-demanding, the brazen and the multicolored, in short to that from which art had hitherto taken its start and which was intensified further in the baroque.[17] Whoever holds such words of Luther before himself will not for a moment doubt where he is to place Rembrandt and also Von Gebhardt and Uhde. Even though Rembrandt may have belonged to a sect, which by the way is not proved, it is nevertheless apparent that he realized what Luther desired. Even without conscious reference to Luther this was possible for him because the fundamental Protestant religious feeling, as soon as it was clear about its own nature, by itself produced the artistic taste that delighted in paradox. So it has certainly been Protestantism that broke the path for the representation of the "contemptible" in art, always, of course, under the condition that in the lowly a spiritual content must appear. But it is not necessary in art, always and in every object, to utter the best and most profound thoughts. It is also a

part of the nature of Protestantism to enjoy
the simply genuine, that which is at home in a
small room, that which is natural for man.
Here it could relate itself to moods that had
already been present in art at an earlier date.
Yet, as is obvious from the paintings of Stein-
hausen and L. Richter, among the later painters, it succeeded even in this case in contribut-
ing something new.

The Reformation, in fact, enriched all areas
of culture. But has it not exhausted its strength
with what it has accomplished to date? Many
would have feared this before the [First]
World War, under the impression that, together with religion in general, the Reformation, too, had lost its power to win a following.
Today a turn in the road seems to be appearing.
The feeling for religion is growing among us.
But the danger threatens that the new movement will lose its way in superstition and utopia.
If ever, we need Luther today to make us
healthy. But one thing must not be forgotten.
The convincing power of the Reformation
rested on the vigor with which it instilled
ethical concepts. And this is the area of most
serious damage today. Consciences everywhere
are confused. In Germany as in other nations.
Only when sober reflection returns at this point

may one hope for a renewal of our nation. But then it will also demonstrate—I believe this confidently—that the Reformation is not at the end, but only at the beginning of its world-wide effect.

NOTES

Scholarly customs for footnote citations vary from country to country as well as from one generation to another. In addition certain conventions for the standard editions of Luther's works have become widely accepted. Karl Holl, moreover, assuming among his readers familiarity as well as access to the sources and knowledge of the Latin of the Reformers, used an extremely abbreviated form of citation. The following abbreviations appear in the footnotes:

CR: CORPUS REFORMATORUM. The citations from Melanchthon and Calvin's works are from this great collection of the works of these Reformers.

EA: The Erlangen edition of Luther's works. The older collection, probably used primarily for texts not yet available in the Weimar edition, which was replacing it.

Enders, BRIEFWECHSEL: Luther's correspondence. The Weimar volumes of Luther's correspondence were not published during Holl's lifetime.

TR: The Weimar edition of Luther's Table Talk.

WA: The Weimar edition of Luther's works. Holl cites by volume (Roman numerals) and part (if the volume appeared in more than one part; Arabic numbers), page and line.

RGG: RELIGION IN GESCHICHTE UND GEGENWART. A major German reference work in the field of religion and its relationships to contemporary society. Holl's references are to articles by Troeltsch in the first edition.

Where the translators were aware of and had access to existing English texts, they consulted these. All translators' notes appear in square brackets [ ]. They have cited the place where a passage may be found in existing translations when it was possible to find such passages. In addition, they translated titles of certain important sources even though no English text is available. The following abbreviations are used:

Am. Ed.: The new American edition of Luther's works in English being brought out jointly by the Concordia Publication House, St. Louis, and the Muhlenberg Press, Philadelphia.

Lenker: THE PRECIOUS AND SACRED WRITING OF MARTIN LUTHER, edited by John N. Lenker. Minneapolis, 1903-10.

Philadelphia: WORKS OF MARTIN LUTHER. Philadelphia, 1915-32.

The translators and the publisher have deleted a number of Holl's notes which were only peripheral to his argument and which in their judgment would be of minor interest to the readers of this book.

I. RELIGION AND SECULAR LIFE

[1] This point of view is taken quite vehemently by E. Fueter in his *Geschichte des europäischen Staatensystems von 1492-1559* (*History of European Systems of State, 1492-1559*). (Munich and Leipzig, 1919.) In it the Reformation is purposely omitted. But even Johannes Haller in his lecture on the reasons for the Reformation, delivered in Tübingen in 1917, shows a similar attitude. His evaluation of the Reformation is based on two axioms: (1) the constantly repeated phrase that "most of what Luther stated and requested had actually already been stated and requested before him"; and (2) the assertion that "Luther's appearance sparked the Reformation not because he denied the doctrine of Rome on absolution and grace, but because he rebelled against the power of the Church."

[2] One can condense Luther's entire work into one single idea: he reasserted reality as opposed to the "as if" of Catholicism. Just as he fought against the "as if" in religion—such as the high esteem of the priest, *as if*

God spoke through him and through his office; or "humility" and "obedience" toward superiors of the Church, *as if* this in itself constituted humility and obedience to God— so he did also in the realm of ethics. Hence his rejection of the "good opinion," which conceives of a certain work (or a certain suffering *as if* it were of service to God or brought him a sacrifice).

[3] Of course, whether this desire for pleasure should be permitted to play a part in religion or morality is an entirely different question.

[4] WA X 3, 380, 5 ff.

[5] WA XL 1, 410, 3.

[6] WA XI, 267, 1 ff.: "If now your lord or temporal superior bids you to believe thus or so or to put aside your books you shall say Lucifer is not worthy to sit beside God. Dear Lord, I am bound to obey you with body and goods, command me according to the measure of your power on earth and I will obey. But if you command me to surrender my faith and my books then I will not obey . . . for I tell you where you do not oppose him, but make way for him so that he takes your faith or your books then you have truly denied God. . . . Not a page, not a letter shall they surrender on pain of loss of their salvation, for whoever does so surrenders Christ into the hands of Herod, for they act like Herod as

murderers of Christ." [Trans.: "Secular Authority," Philadelphia, III, 257.]

[7] TR II, 299, 4 ff.: "God has ordained that all men eat their bread in the sweat of their brow and this He has ordained so that whoever does not wish this burden may be forced to bear the burden of a bad conscience."

[8] WA XII, 464, 9: "The old ass is flesh and blood who must be compelled and driven so that he works and nevertheless is lazy."

[9] Enders, BRIEFWECHSEL [*Correspondence*], III, 219, 61: "But may I not ultimately be burdensome and troublesome to these men, for I would want no one to be burdened by me."

[10] WA XV, 302, 33: "For Christians are brothers and one does not forsake the other. Nor is any so lazy and shameless that without working he would rely on another's goods and work and would consume another's possessions in indolence. [Trans.: "On Commerce and Usury," Philadelphia, IV, 23.]

EA 9, 319: "For this is the correct interpretation of the commandment 'Thou shalt not steal' that is, you shall support yourself with your own work so that you have something of your own and can also give to the needy person. This is your duty and where you do not do so God will judge you as no Christian, but a thief and a robber; first because you are living in idleness and are not providing for yourself with your own work, but are taking another's blood and sweat, secondly because you deprive your neighbor of that which you are duty bound to give him."

[11] WA VI, 36, 23: "Is not to be understood as some think that one should throw him one's cloak after one's coat, but that one should also let the cloak go, not to resist nor to be impatient about it nor to attempt to recover it." Ibid., 37, 14: "For this is a Christian and brotherly faithfulness that you take him by surprise and confront him who is wronging you with his injustice and God's judgment, and you owe it to him to say also 'Hold on, you are taking my coat and this thing and that thing, you must answer for it whether you are doing right.' And this you must do not primarily because of the injury you have received nor to threaten him, but to warn him and remind him of his destruction. If he does not heed you, let be what will be and let him take more." [Trans.: "On Usury" (1520), Philadelphia, IV, 37 and 38.]

[12] WA LI, 383, 1 ff.: "Furthermore every man here does not mean the one who has enough or can have enough for (particularly nowadays) there are innumerable no-good rascals who pretend to be poor, needy and beggarly and deceive the people; to these one should

let Master John give his alms with strictness and dispatch . . . there are also even more of these lazy persons who are strong, healthy and able to work and serve and support themselves . . . Christ never commanded us to give to these." [*"An die Pfarrherren, wider den Wucher zu predigen"* (1540) ("To the Clergy, an Admonition to Preach Against Usury" [1540]).]

EA 8, 309: "As it is still necessary among Christians that those who are truly poor (*not lazy beggers or tramps*) are to be provided for and supported."

[13] WA XV, 303, 10: "For you are first of all and chiefly responsible to provide wife, child, and dependents with what they need and must not divert from them what is owing to them from you. [Trans.: "On Commerce and Usury," Philadelphia, IV, 23-4.]

[14] TR II, 647, 6: "For at times everyone wanted to become rich off me, there was no end to begging." [*Table Talk,* Sept. 28-Nov. 13, 1523.]

WA XX, 714, 3: "And we are frequently mocked by robust beggers."

WA XXVI, 639, 14: "This year I myself have been so befouled and tempted by such vagabonds and smooth talkers, more than I care to admit." ["The Mischief Done by Fake Beggers" (1528).]

[15] WA VI, 272, 25: "Without faith liberality is worthless; it is rather a careless squandering of money." [Trans.: "Sermon on Good Works" (1520), Philadelphia II, 280.]

[16] WA LI, 394, 4: "But this is a difficult and rare lending, as was said above of giving, that I should lend with a simple heart not desiring security for it or binding my neighbor with it or making him my dependent. . . . In conclusion such misery and heartache that a person would like to play God for another comes from the apple in Paradise when Adam and Eve in the devil's name wanted to be gods." ["To the Clergy, An Admonition to Preach Against Usury" (1540).]

II. EFFECTS ON POLITICAL AND ECONOMIC LIFE

[1] Here again, I want to reassert that it was not the Baptists who posed this question for the first time.

[2] Troeltsch's article on natural law (*RGG* IV, 697 ff.), in which he summarizes his point of view, moves me at almost every point to disagreement. Here I do not want to repeat once again what I have said elsewhere (*"Der Neubau der Sittlichkeit"*) about the am-

biguity of Troeltsch's concept of *lex naturae,* about his conception of the difference between church and sect, and about the concept of reason in Luther. But where can one find in Luther and Melanchthon the shading between the *absolute* natural law of man's first state and the *relative* natural law of the state of sin which Troeltsch ascribes to them? Where does either of them make even the slightest attempt to describe man's first state more closely—and the law presumably valid then—and to derive anything from that? When they indeed in their justification of the state take the fact of sin—and not *only* that —into account can one then immediately say that they have *derived* the state from sin? Certainly such a statement as: "Here the right of force is proclaimed as the rebellious peasants most thoroughly came to feel," may not be made. In doing so Troeltsch, and others as well, has completely forgotten that Luther demanded exactly the same of the Protestant lords over against the Emperor as he required of the peasants. Can one then really assert that Luther has in this instance proclaimed the Emperor's right to use force? Troeltsch finally says about Luther's natural law: "It is at every point a crude, raw, and aphoristic theory." I find Luther's (real) view less "raw" than those of Hobbes, toward which one otherwise shows a certain respect.

[3] CR XXI, 991: "Thus Paludanus says that a political order of such greatness has its origin from God, since the understanding and knowledge of the laws of nature was imposed upon man, because He decided that this order among men is necessary. As true as this opinion may be he has not said enough about the cause of civil society or of empires. For by no means can honorable laws and civil society be preserved by human councils and physical strength alone. Therefore we know that this order is established and confirmed by the voice of God and indeed is sustained by Him." [From the *Loci Communes,* 3rd ed., 1559.]

[4] CR XVI, 438: "And in this precept authority was established: honor thy father and thy mother. For this was commanded in obedience toward one's elders. Those speak falsely who give such great authority to the consent of the people, as Occam says: for the rulers by right command even those that are unwilling and rightfully take possession of the power not only by election or by vote and consent of the people, but also by legitimate war, by conscription of soldiers, by legitimate succession, etc." [From the "Commentary on Aristotle's *Politics*" (1530).]

[5] WA XVI, 537, 12: "This comes from the weak administration in Germany." [From "Sermons on Exodus" (1524-7).]

WA XVII 1, 149, 14: "We have neither emperor nor king. Every man does as he wishes. Princes and magistrates do not punish their subjects until God throws one crowd of them upon the other." [From "Sermons of the Year 1525"; preached on March 24, 1525.]

WA XXV, 505, 20: "This is why things are going thus in Germany, so that there is no order; but if one would occasionally go through the country and beat the one or the other over the head, there would be peace." [From "Sermons on Leviticus and Numbers."]

[6] EA 53, 325: "Thus it is not good to rule with the dislike, resistance and enmity of the subjects; it also will not last."

[7] WA XVIII, 437, 33: "For it cannot endure when a people does not love its ruler, but has only to fear him." [From "Preface to Karlstadt's Apology" (1525).]

[8] EA 53, 302: "For your lordship may well perceive that one cannot today rule the world with force alone and . . . if there were no teachers and preachers temporal power would not long survive."

WA XIX, 440, 7 ff.: "Thus it is necessary

that one does not act with force alone as is currently done, but also with reason, for pure force without reason cannot endure and keeps the subjects in eternal hatred against the government."

[9] WA XXX, 2, 128, 25 ff.: "He (that is, the Turk) is like a Muentzer radical for he roots out all government and permits no temporal estates (such as lords, barons, rulers, noblemen and other vassals) but is the sole ruler of everything in his country, makes only monetary grants, but bestows no lands or positions of authority." [Trans.: "War with the Turks" (1529), Philadelphia, V, 181.]

[10] Not in England either. There the Catholics were persecuted because they were suspected of high treason, ever since the Gunpowder Plot. Cromwell did not tolerate them because they were unreliable, because their yes does not mean yes and their no is not no.

[11] I want to stress that Calvin, too, whom historical literature commonly treats as a fanatic enemy of Catholicism, adopted Luther's attitude. However, one should bear in mind that among Luther's statements condemned by Leo X, the thirty-third reads as follows: *Haereticos comburi est contra voluntatem spiritus.*

[12] This holds specifically also for the colony founded by Baltimore, which the Catholics

always praise. It is no proof that the Catholic Church first granted tolerance, for the Catholic *Church* had no part whatsoever in it. The "tolerance" had obvious economic grounds. For a purely Catholic colony a sufficient number of settlers would never have been found. In so far as tolerance came into the matter at all it is not to be found on the side of the Catholic Church, but of the English king.

[13] WA XXXI 1, 197, 9 and 29: "It is not a revolutionary act to punish the government if it is done in the manner described here, namely that it is done through a divinely ordained office and through the word of God openly, freely and sincerely." [Trans.: "Exposition of the 82nd Psalm," Am. Ed., XIII, 50.]

WA XII, 334, 16 (on I Peter 2:17): "He does not say that one should have a high regard for kings and magistrates, but that one ought nevertheless to honor them." [Trans.: Lenker, III, 123.]

WA XV, 44, 34: "Princes and lords ought to do it, but they must ride around in sledges, and drink, and take part in masquerades; they are burdened with high and important business in cellar, kitchen, and bedroom." [Trans.: "To the Councilmen of All Cities in Germany That They Establish Christian

Schools" (1524). Philadelphia, IV, 121.]

[14] CR XXI, 1002: "I have, however, discussed the subject more fully so that I may remind young people to accustom their minds to loving the political order and being reminded they may perceive that in this the wisdom, justice, and goodness of God toward mankind is discernible. It is customary for young people to show keen understanding in their censure of civil law and custom. But we know that cynical wisdom and impudence must be renounced and abominated." With special application to preachers, p. 1008: "However, they know that good administration of the judiciary and of public business is to be commended to the other occupations, and they recall the customary precept that everyone knows his own Sparta." [From the *Loci Communes,* 3rd ed.]

[15] It seems worth noting, if one considers the history of Saxony, also especially his opinion concerning inheritance. TR II, 427, 28: "Moses, however, had the best arrangement, where the first born had such a great measure of kingly function but the rest were subjects. . . . It is the same today in the East and it would be the soundest system for us."

[16] CR XVI, 442: "Here the power of the kings is limited by laws and some freedom is allowed to the people. Just as in Germany, *be-*

cause the rulers make use of Roman law, all the subjects everywhere are not on that account slaves in a proper sense." P. 446: "Already at some time other nations have complained rightfully regarding their laws, certainly at this time it is least fitting for the Germans to complain since we make use of Roman law, *which is full of humanity and justice,* which has been written by men most experienced in ruling the state, which has brought this nation whose savagery was once the greatest, to a milder and a more humane life." [From the "Commentary on Aristotle's *Politics.*]

[17] At any rate, it is noteworthy that the powers of the Counter Reformation began to lay the basis for absolutism much earlier. Maximilian of Bavaria and Ferdinand II of Austria utilized the fight against the Reformation to put an end to liberty in their countries.

[18] Of Luther's many utterances that could be presented here I choose WA XIV, 550, 23 ff.: "Because at the same time the office of the magistrate is to bear the hardships, burdens, and quarrels of the people in order that he may acknowledge himself to be their servant, not their master; this is what love requires. They do evil who in their magistracy indeed seek advantages quickly and secretly, that the people may rather serve them and they may

derive advantages for their inordinate desires from the misfortunes of the people." ["Lectures on Deuteronomy" (1523-4).]

[19] CR XVI, 438: "Then there are certain persons who have argued that the Roman emperor is the absolute ruler of the whole world and have cited the evangelist Luke 2:1 and also Matt. 22:21, etc. So therefore we shall perceive that neither the Roman pontiff nor Caesar is the monarch of the whole world, but that individual kings rule over their own territories just as there have always been separate kingdoms in the world." ["Commentary on Aristotle's *Politics*."]

[20] Compare the penetrating essay by Meinecke, "*Die Lehre von den Interessen der Staaten im Frankreich Richelieus*," *Historische Zeitschrift*, Vol. 123, pp. 14 ff.

[21] *Gedanken und Erinnerungen*, Vol. 2, p. 46: "I replied it was not for us to discharge the duties of a judge, but to practice German politics; Austria's competitive struggle against us no more deserved punishment than ours against Austria. . . . I repeated that it was not for us to exercise retaliatory justice, but to act politically."

[22] Compare what Bismarck stated in his last conference of ministers, *Gedanken und Erinnerungen*, Vol. 3, p. 166: "Russia needs the existence of France as we do that of Austria

as a major power." Could an English, American, or French statesman even have considered such a thought?

[23] Compare the investigation of Karl Müller, entitled "*Luthers Ausserungen über das Recht des bewaffneten Widerstands gegen den Kaiser*" ("*Luther's Statements about the Right of Armed Resistance against the Emperor*"), *Sitzungs-Bericht der Bayrischen Akademie*, 1915.

[24] In this connection I think of the frequently repeated designation of the estates as ephors, which, so far as I can see, was introduced by Melanchthon. Cf. *CR* XVI, 440: "Such kings are not at all autocratic or absolute: that is, they do not have supreme power to such an extent that no one is allowed to judge them or to oppose their actions. And, moreover, there are such kingdoms today. For they have laws and they have guardians. In Germany they are the electors, in France certain leaders of the parliamentary senate, just as the ephors of the kings. But in one plan they have more power, in another they have less." Melanchthon, in contrast to Luther, nevertheless did not refrain from including natural law in his judgment. ["Commentary on Aristotle's *Politics*."]

[25] Compare the thorough book by Kurt Wolzendorff, *Staatsrecht und Naturrecht in der*

Lehre vom Widerstandsrecht des Volkes gegen rechtswidrige Ausübung der Staatsgewalt (Untersuchung zur deutschen Staats- und Rechtsgeschichte, 1916). I value in this book particularly the clear recognition of the transition of historic to natural law within the movement of the Reformation.

[26] I emphasize especially that Calvin, too, just as Luther, made "reason," i.e., ultimately love, the highest standard for all laws and systems of law. CR *Calvini opera* I, 237. "Moral law, therefore, which is contained in two parts, of which one simply commands us to worship God with pure faith and piety, the other to embrace men with sincere love, is the true and eternal rule of righteousness, prescribed to men of all ages and nations." Ibid., p. 238; "Let us consider as is proper these two things in all laws: the constitution and equity of the law, on the reason of which the constitution itself depends. Now since the law of God which we call the moral law, is not other than a declaration of natural law and of that conscience which has been engraved upon the minds of men by God, in all of this the rule of equity has been prescribed. Therefore this ought to be alone the scope and rule and end of all laws." [From the *Institutes of the Christian Religion,* IV, Ch. 20, Sec. 15, 16.]

[27] CR *Calvini opera* I, 248: "For if those who are now appointed popular magistrates to keep within bounds the desires of kings such as were formally the ephors who were set against the Lacedaemonians or the tribunes of the people against the Roman consuls, or the demarchs against the Athenian senate and even with the strong power which the state now has, the three estates perform in the individual kingdoms when they hold their assemblies, I do not forbid them to this extent to protest against the violent willfullness of kings in the discharge of their duty, for if weakly they let pass unnoticed the violent rages of their kings and their insults to the common people I affirm that their dissimulation is *nefarious perfidy,* because they *fraudulently betray* the freedom of the people of which they are the acknowledged guardians appointed by the ordinance of God." [Ibid., Sec. 31.]

[28] CR *Calvini opera* I, 1105 ff.: "Indeed even the magistrates ought to be intent upon this with the greatest diligence lest they allow the freedom for which they are appointed as guardians to diminish in some way, not to say to be violated. If in this respect, they are lazier and little disturbed, they are faithless in their duty and traitors to their country."

[29] CR *Calvini opera* I, 247: "For sometimes

from His own servents He raises up public avengers and gives them His mandate to inflict punishment on unrighteous despotism and to deliver from their wretched misfortune a people oppressed by unjust measures, sometimes He accomplishes this purpose by the fury of men who think and attempt something different. For if the correction of unrestrained despotism is the vengeance of God let us not conclude therefore that it is entrusted to us who have no other command than that of obeying and suffering. I am speaking always of private individuals." [Ibid., Sec. 30, 31.]

[30] The best interpretation of these circumstances is found in Karl Müller's *Kirchengeschichte,* II, 2nd par., pp. 266 ff. I agree with Müller specifically in that the influence of the Continental Anabaptists is much smaller than is generally supposed. Nevertheless, the more recent "autobiographies" of these sects should be read with some caution. All of them attempt—at least up to the [First] World War—to deny their connection with the old Anabaptists, claiming that they had never had anything to do with Münzer and the Münster group.

[31] CR *Calvini opera* I, 228: "That distinction must be kept in mind . . . lest falling into a mistake that happens to many, injudiciously

we mix together two things which have an entirely different nature. For some, when they hear liberty promised in the gospel . . . think that they cannot take any enjoyment from their liberty as long as they see any authority set over them. . . . But in fact he who has learned to distinguish between the body and the soul, between this present and changing life and that future and eternal one, will not think it difficult to believe that the spiritual kingdom of Christ and the order of the civil state are very different." [From the *Institutes,* IV, Ch. 20, Sec. 1.]

[32] The index of the publications of the Parker Society offers the simplest statement (s.v. "England," p. 298): "England's privileges, God's great mercies to it." Here are some other passages: Becon, *Prayers and Other Pieces,* p. 11: "That God yet once again is come on visitation to this church of England . . . and made it a glorious church." Ibid., p. 206: "What realm since the apostle's time was ever so abundantly replenished with the knowledge of Christ's gospel?" Bradford, *Sermons,* p. 13: "[Blessings] as no people heretofore hath had." Norden, *Progress of Piety,* p. 39: "But also in regard of the daily experience of her most sacred government, which is such and so gracious as the like benefit hath not been extended to any

nation before us." *Private Prayers of the Reign of Queen Elizabeth*, p. 477: "For giving us such, so wise, so zealous, so godly and careful, governors of thy chosen church of England."—As H. Oncken, *Sitz.-Ber. Heidelberg Akademie* (1922), has shown, the beginnings of this self-awareness are already visible in Thomas More's *Utopia*. But the awareness of a mission toward the entire world resulted only from the addition of the religious concept.

[33] H. Oncken, op. cit., pointed out very ably that what the English call "Machiavellianism" in the German is actually the German love for truth and the distaste for pious phrases where in reality other motivations are, at least partly, at play.

[34] Again and again the issue of the personal relation between Luther and Melanchthon becomes apparent. In 1540 Luther wrote his conscience-shaking work "To the Clergy to Preach on Usury" and in the meantime Melanchthon was training his students for quite different viewpoints in his philosophical and theological lectures. Is it conceivable that Luther noticed nothing of all this? And yet he was silent about this difference as about others (territorial church administration and the like) not only publicly but also in his *Table Talk*. This really gives the full picture

of the high esteem Luther had for Melanchthon and how much he, presumably so insistent on being right, endured from his friend.

[35] CR XVI, 133: "However, the customary rule stands that the decision of the law in civil matters should be followed and that the Christian is permitted to make use of the laws and contracts which are approved by the laws." [From "Epitome of Moral Philosophy" (1538).]

Ibid., 429: "We reply briefly that the Christian is allowed to make use of contracts which the laws approve and decide, just as the Christian is permitted to make use of other political arrangements. [From "Commentary on Aristotle's *Politics*."]

[36] When one reads the customary portrayals of Calvin's views one can only ask oneself again how long it has been since someone has read Calvin himself on these matters. Even Troeltsch only restates the customary point of view. Compare for example his articles "Natural Law" (*Religion in Geschichte und Gegenwart*, IV, 702): "Calvin made a further change in economic doctrine in that he declared the taking of interest and commerce to be natural rights and therefore also Christian. In a commercial city like Geneva nothing else was possible, and later the

Dutchman Salmasius gave it a thorough scientific foundation."

[37] CR *Calvini opera* XXIV, 682: "Nor indeed does that artful theory of Aristotle's stand that usury was contrary to nature since money is sterile and does not bring forth money. For the man whom I have called a cheat will be able to make an abundant profit by carrying on a business with money that belongs to another. The purchaser reaps from the estate and he will gather in the vintage." In ibid., XXVIII, 118 and 119 he speaks of the statement that "money cannot possibly give birth to money" as a frivolous or puerile argument.

[38] CR *Calvini opera* XL, 432: "Since otherwise men can not carry on business among themselves." Ibid., XXVIII, 117: "It would be necessary to stop all business completely: it would not be at all lawful to practice trade as is now done."

[39] CR *Calvini opera* XL, 431: "And certainly the money lender will always be a robber, that is, that one is a robber who makes a profit from lending money at interest. . . . But it is another thing to lend money at interest than to receive a profit. For when any one has set up a money changer's counter, he now makes use of his trade in the same way that the farmer puts his labor into cul-

tivating his fields, but it will be possible for some one to make a profit who nevertheless will not lend money at interest."

[40] CR *Calvini opera* XXIV, 681: "If, however, something must be said with finality on this matter itself, the definition must be chosen from no other source than from the common rule of justice and especially from the expression of Christ [i.e., not from the "natural law"!] on which the law and prophets depend. Matt. 7:12." Ibid., XXVIII, 122: "Here, then, is what we need to keep in mind: to know that when we pose the question whether all forms of usury are lawful, it is necessary to consider not only this remark about usury, but it is also necessary to consider the intention of God. But now to understand it well, it is necessary to reach the justice which He showed us in his law. And even we shall hear what our Lord Jesus Christ said. "Matt. 7:12." Ibid., XXIV, 680: "Everyone without exception must refrain from usury and other exploitation and justice must also be preserved toward strangers. Indeed the members of the household of faith come first (just as Paul commands that we do well especially to them, Gal. 6:10). However the common society of mankind demands that we may not seek to become rich at the expense of others."

[41] CR *Calvini opera* XXIV, 682: "If the transaction is with the rich, the right of lending money at interest is allowed without restraint."

[42] CR *Calvini opera* XXIV, 680: "This is the chief of the first principles, that the power of the wealthy shall be sufficient for him to lift up the poor who has fallen down and strengthen him who is tottering. The precept for lending without interest is added since, although it is a political matter, it depends nevertheless upon the role of love: because it is hardly possible to achieve something since the poor are impoverished by the exactions of the money lender and their blood is almost sucked out." Ibid., X, 431: "It will always be a crime to take interest from the poor."

[43] CR *Calvini opera* XXVIII, 121: "For look at the law, which will be for five per cent. Now it is a general law in as much as the magistrates are quite unable to give a set rate for each case: but they will order that one take five per cent. And why? For purposes of commerce, so that one cannot take more than that. Now is that to say perhaps that it is always right to take five per cent? Not at all."

[44] Documentation for this and subsequent remarks on the subject are to be found in my

essay, "*Die Frage des Zinsnehmens in der reformierten Kirch,*" *Festgabe für K. Müller* (Tübingen, 1922), pp. 178 ff. (*Gesammelte Aufsätze zur Kirchengeschichte,* III, 1928, pp. 385 ff.).

[45] Max Weber, who was in the habit of reading the sources thoroughly himself, pointed out these facts. But he is mistaken, when he believes that Calvin's position was "unambiguous." It is also necessary to examine the individual points more thoroughly than he did.

[46] I want to stress especially that the Synod of Emden (1571) emphatically prohibited both the accumulation of money as a means to acquire more money and the compounding of interest. Salmasius, too, considered the refinements in the art of interest-taking as something unethical.

[47] See, for instance, the interpretation of the Eighth Commandment in the Great Westminster Catechism, which—and this differentiates the emerging capitalist spirit from that of the old Calvinism—always stresses the simultaneous duty toward charity.

[48] In his recent revision Max Weber made an effort to qualify the demonstration even more carefully than the first time. One could only wish that just these qualifications would now be universally noted. Nothing has damaged

the impartial estimation of Weber's proposition so much as the vulgar applications that his theories have received from the theologians and secular historians. Today one may read side by side with reference to Max Weber that Calvinism in distinction to Lutheranism (which left things as they were) boldly transformed the social and economic relationships, or conversely that Calvinism even more than Lutheranism recognized the *autonomy* of secular life. Both are presumably "this-worldly asceticism." Or one learns that Calvinism developed greater economic energy because for Calvinism owing to the certainty of predestination the questions of personal religion were completely solved, or at the same time again the opposite, that the greater economic energy arose rather out of the abiding inner unrest which anxiety over one's election caused. Thus everything is happily mixed up. For my part I have avoided the term "this-worldly asceticism" because it has many meanings and is not significant for distinguishing the confessions. For even Catholicism knows a this-worldly asceticism. I call to mind only the examination of particulars.

[49] I would not emphasize the ideas of "election" and "perseverance" as much as Weber, depending on Schneckenburger, has done. More

important, it seems to me, both for the religious self-consciousness of the Puritan and
for the genesis of the capitalistic spirit, is the
striving for perfection. It gives birth to the
calculating frame of mind.

[50] This can even be established in terms of
speech. W. Franz (*Der Wert der englischen
Kultur,* Tübingen, 1913, p. 4) has nicely emphasized that since the rise of Puritanism
compounds with "self" have increased remarkably in English and that particularly
words like "self-respect," "self-esteem,"
"self-control," "self-education" belong primarily to this period of development.

[51] It is still debatable to what degree Karlstadt
is to be named along with Luther. In the first
Wittenberg relief regulations I would more
confidently than Pallas (*ZKG. der Provinz
Sachsen,* Vol. 12, pp.1 ff., 100 ff., and Vol. 13,
pp. 1 ff.) trace the idea back to Luther. But
the plan also to support the middle class
could nevertheless also be traced to Karlstadt.

[52] Cf. Enders VII, 255, 44 ff.: "There are in
the churches of Christ upright deacons who
have regard for the poor . . . care of the
poor, correct administration of the community chest."

[53] WA XII, 693, 33: "It would be good if one
still began, provided the persons for it were

at hand, to divide a town like this one into four or five districts, assign a minister or deacon to each, who would divide the goods, take care of the sick, and look after the needy. But we do not have the men for it; therefore I do not dare begin until the Lord God makes some Christians." [From "Sermon on St. Stephen's Day" (1523).]

[54] For this and the following comments see Holl, *"Thomas Chalmers und die Anfänge der kirchlich-sozialen Bewegung," Zeitschrift für Theologie und Kirche* (1912) (*Gesammelte Aufsätze zur Kirchengeschichte*, III, 1928, pp. 433 ff.).

[55] One dare not treat the Lutheranism of this period as a unity, as if in its totality it had no understanding for social problems, or at best was concerned with them only in a "patriarchal" sense. It is sufficient to mention the name of Löhe.

[56] For the guilt of social democracy see the very trustworthy document by Heinrich Cunow, *Die Marxsche Geschichts-, Gesellschafts- und Staatstheorie* (1920). Cunow explained the tactics of the Social Democrats—to oppose even such plans by the government that they should have supported —by pointing out that Marx had not left behind any program whatsoever about the state, since he innocently assumed that the

state would simply disintegrate into just society; so that "vulgar Marxism" had to refer back to pre-Marxian English concepts of the eighteenth century in order to have any concept of the state at all.

[57] I do not understand how Weber could assert the proposition (*Ges. Auf. z. Rel.-Soziol.*, p. 101, and notes), since then often repeated by others, that in Calvinism love of neighbor acquired "a peculiar factual-impersonal character," and even "the humanity of the relationship to the neighbor so to speak died out." I can explain these sentences by Weber only by the fact that here as in his whole analysis he had only American examples before him. His verdict may fit America. I would not know where to begin to exhaust the evidence for the opposite in Calvinism. I believe that in view of what follows in the text I can spare myself this. The entire line of evidence from Chalmers would be pointless if it had not become a part of his flesh and blood and if he could not assume this even in others, that love of neighbor must have a completely personal character.

[58] That this was not only Chalmers's personal attitude but also reflected the general concepts of the Reformed Church can be seen from the principles of the Quakers (*Christian Discipline of the Society of Friends*, III,

Ch. 16, p. 84) : "We have ever esteemed the duty of ministring to the wants of the poor as one of the primary obligations . . . whilst enjoining the duty of charity on those who are of ability to extend it, we would remind our poor Friends that it is their duty by frugality and industry to use their strenuous endeavours to maintain themselves and their families and by small savings in time of health to provide for sickness and old age, so as not to be dependent on others."

III. EFFECTS ON EDUCATION, HISTORY, PHILOSOPHY, POETRY, AND ART

[1] Enders, VII, 255, 19: "And to preserve such doctrine attention is given very seriously that schools for boys and girls for the proper education of youth are founded and maintained."

[2] EA 53, 401: "I thought to use you to teach young girls and through you commend this work to others as an example. You shall have your bed and board with me."

[3] WA XXX 2, 586, 7 ff.: "But I hold that it is the duty of the government to compel its subjects to keep their children in school."

[Trans.: "A Sermon on Keeping Children in School" (1530), Philadelphia, IV, 177.]

[4] Compare his warning to the Bohemians (*WA* XI, 455, 27): "I would plead that you do not disdain languages, but since you could easily do so, have your preachers and gifted boys as well learn good Latin, Greek, and Hebrew. For I am experiencing how these languages help immeasurably in a clear understanding of the divine writings."

[5] WA XIX, 74, 4: "For I would under no circumstances take the Latin language entirely out of the service, for youth is my chief concern. And if it were possible and Greek and Hebrew were as familiar to us as Latin and contained as much good music and song, we would hold mass, sing and read, on successive Sundays in all four languages, German, Latin, Greek and Hebrew." [Trans.: "The German Mass and Order of Service" (1526), Philadelphia, VI, 172.]

[6] WA XV, 47, 13: "But the exceptional pupils who give promise of becoming skilled teachers, preachers and holders of other spiritual positions should be kept at school longer or altogether dedicated to a life of study." [Trans.: "To the Councilmen of All Cities in Germany that They Establish and Maintain Christian Schools" (1524), Philadelphia, IV, 124.]

[7] WA XXVI, 239, 29 ff.: "When the children have become well-versed in grammar one should select the most gifted and form a third group." [From "Instruction for the Visitation of Pastors" (1528).]

[8] Cf. also his thesis, EA v. arg. 4, 336, Thesis 11: "The philosophy of the natural qualities and properties of things (quite unknown to the sophists) is useful to sacred theology."

[9] E. Fueter's treatment (in his *Geschichte der neueren Historiographie*, Munich and Berlin, 1911) is strongly influenced by his personal taste, which also narrows his knowledge considerably. That he treats the Jesuits with love but overlooks or minimizes the accomplishments of the Reformation is also a reflection of his personal taste.

[10] It is one of those judgments that are carried over from book to book that Sebastian Franck, at that time in lonely greatness, had stood for the "relative point of view" which supposedly enabled him to pass fair judgment even on the Turks. Unquestionably Franck, who had no specifically religious point of view, was able to spot weaknesses in all existing sects; and whoever shares Franck's attitude toward religion is entitled to praise him. Seen from an ethical point of view, it is—as has already been stated—a far greater accomplishment that Luther was able, despite

the absoluteness of his own point of view and despite his extreme opposition to the Catholic Church, to appreciate her in some measure. And as far as the Turks are concerned, Luther often stressed their positive traits (despite his adamant fight against their religion). He also insisted that in order to judge the Turks one must go to the source, i.e., read the Koran.

[11] Compare Holl, *Gesammelte Aufsätze zur Kirchengeschichte*, I, *Luther*, pp. 222 ff.; also the excellent essays by E. Hirsch, "*Luther und Nietzsche*," *Jahrbuch der Luthergesellschaft* (1921), pp. 61 ff., and Chr. Schrempf, *Diesseits und Jenseits von Gut und Böse* (1921), and *Friedrich Nietzsche* (1922). Both recognized the direct line that leads from Paul via Luther to Nietzsche.

[12] Compare also the conclusion of Schrempf, *Friedrich Nietzsche*, p. 128: "Zarathustra is a higher man. Despite everything! But Zarathustra traps himself hopelessly in the 'It Was.' To redeem the past in man and re-create all 'It Was' until the will speaks: 'But this is how I wanted it! This is how I will it!' —This is impossible. . . . If man comes to recognize this he turns from the path of Zarathustra to that of Jesus."

[13] Compare the deeply searching lectures by Gustav Roethe, *Martin Luthers Bedeutung*

für die deutsche Literatur (Berlin, 1916).

[14] Our aesthetes speak of a "poverty of Puritanism" as opposed to the "wealth of the Catholic soul." One is only capable of such a judgment if one has never read a Puritan book of edification, and if one has never heard of the influence of Puritanism on English literature.

[15] In this, German Pietism differs sharply from English Puritanism. How very little one hears from Bunyan or Fox about the world in which they lived.

[16] Compare Morf, *Geschichte der französischen Literatur* (1898), pp. 198 ff. However, French Calvinism later became quite suspicious of miracle plays.

[17] In my essay *"Die geistlichen Ubungen des Ignatius von Loyola"* (*Sammlung gemeinverständlicher Vorträge,* Tübingen, 1906, I demonstrated that the taste of the baroque was also founded on a basic religious mood, the spirit of *exercitia spiritualia*.